This book is lovingly dedicated to my wife and children,
whose unselfish support over the years has provided me a
sanctuary throughout my intense struggle to achieve innate
awareness, overcome personal and financial setbacks,
and succeed in gaining increased public awareness and
professional recognition for chiropractic.

Contents

Foreword

The experiences shared with you on the following pages have been lived and recorded by a unique and complex individual. He has excelled as both an athlete and a scholar. Although aggressive and competitive, he seeks to live each day with love as his master. Although down-to-earth and practical, he is a very spiritual man with great compassion, who earnestly and unselfishly seeks to love, serve and give out of his own abundance. He is a visionary leader who directs and encourages other to greatness, and inspires them to become a living example of his philosophy of service to humanity.

Dr. Sid Williams' own life would supply ample material for a Horatio Alger "rags to riches" novel. From simple beginnings, he worked his way up the ladder of success one rung at a time by resolving to give himself completely to whatever task he undertook. He discovered for himself at a very young age the great value of such simple habits as belief, focus and persistence. His Lasting Purpose shaped his goals and directed his life. He became a healer of healers, an entrepreneur's entrepreneur, the founder of a university and a spellbinding inspirational speaker. His phenomenal achievements provide the most eloquent testament to his character and to the principles he has developed.

When I first met Dr. Sid Williams over two decades ago, I was profoundly impressed by his brilliance and personal magnetism. He is one of the few people whose vitality and life energy are so intense that his very presence in a room electrifies the atmosphere. I believe his passion for his Lasting Purpose and his strength of focus have made him larger than life itself.

As I have visited his campus over the years to speak to his students, my respect for Dr. Williams has grown in quantum leaps. He has shown that when your purpose is clear, there are no limits to personal success. Most people in his position and with his achievements are ready for retirement. Not Sid Williams! Every time we meet, he shares with me that he is "just beginning." Knowing Dr. Williams has been a constant inspiration.

In *Lasting Purpose,* Dr. Williams proposes not just a path to material success, but a journey to a joyful life. He also teaches that understanding a concept is merely the first step. He shows that it is only when you *apply* what you learn that it truly becomes yours and begins to enhance your life.

Once you discover your own Lasting Purpose, you will unleash a power within that you have not known before. You will see what direction your life should take and learn how to create a larger vision of your future. Fears may remain, but they will not stop you; you will not be sidetracked by the roadblocks to success that may halt others. You will become solution-oriented and have more to give. Your life will be of greater service to you, your family, your community and the world.

Read and enjoy the following pages. Resist the temptation to reject an idea that seems to clash with what you have learned to consider "reality." To the scholar, eager to learn, reality changes as rapidly and as dependably as patterns in the clouds. Stand on your own mountain and seek new vistas. Put your new knowledge to work. Enjoy the new attitudes and habits you adopt. Enjoy the new you, and soon you will find that life itself is a joy. Such is the promise of this book—and you will not be disappointed.

Mark Victor Hansen
coauthor of the *New York Times* bestselling
Chicken Soup for the Soul series

Introduction

It is only by stopping and looking back with a wiser and more experienced eye that we can see the major turning points in our lives. Like canyons, our ultimate shape is largely determined by the material of which we are made and the elements of our environment that pound against us. The pattering rains wear us down a little, but it's the big floods and hailstorms that truly make their mark. These are what we often call turning points.

Where we humans mainly differ from simple clay and rock is that we are able to make choices. We cannot choose our basic nature, of course; neither can we always choose our environment. But once we realize that regardless of this, we are still able to make choices, we can then choose how best to use the talents and attributes we have, whether great or meager. We can also do the best possible job in whatever environment we find ourselves, whether it turns out to be friendly or hostile.

Looking back, I suppose it was good fortune that I was born into one of the most challenging times in this country's history—the Great Depression of the 1930s. It taught me the value of money and gave me an appreciation for hard work. I was about two years old when Black Monday hit.

Even without a formal education, my father had made a fair living as a farmer, peddler and entrepreneur. But the Depression wiped him out financially. My mother and I helped in any way we could. I remember when I was just six or seven years old, my mother would boil peanuts, and I would take them down to the square in the little country town where we lived to sell them.

Later, my folks began farming a small plot of land that my grandmother had left us. But that enterprise ended abruptly. Upon returning from a trip out of town, we found our house burned to the ground. We then moved into a little three-room rental house in East Point, south of Atlanta. The house was so small that the whole family had to sleep in the same room. All of our personal belongings except an old tin tub had been destroyed in the fire. The tub, which we used for bathing, doubled as a dining-room table.

I can remember getting a little, dark blue, checkered jacket from the WPA that my mother wouldn't let me wear outside— everyone would know it was charity, she said. At the time, as people used to say, we were "too poor to paint but too proud to whitewash." I cannot recall having any books in the house, and I never even read a newspaper until I was in high school.

There was a lot of tension in our home because of the lack of money, but our prospects improved around 1937, when we moved into a little community called Oakland City Park, on the southwest side of Atlanta. Thanks to my father's entre-preneurial spirit and my mother's determination and persistence—which were models for me to follow—Dad's consumable products business began to improve steadily. We were never without food and a roof over our heads. Despite all the hardships, both of my parents always encouraged me never to give up once I set out to do something. My mother wanted her child to be the best and would accept nothing less.

This book contains the essence of my philosophy of life, which is encapsulated in the term "Lasting Purpose." As I look back to reconstruct the development of my Lasting Purpose philosophy, I can see now that my philosophical and spiritual development came in somewhat measured steps, each step preparing me to reach the next one. One particular turning point that stands out in my mind is when I was just five or six years old: I made the choice to emulate my movie heroes and to learn to throw a knife. Learning to throw a knife correctly and accurately, while learning to be an innate part of the process, was a very important first step that opened many new doors of adventure for me.

Most of the youngsters in my neighborhood would spend a few frustrating minutes trying to perfect a skill requiring repetitive activity, then give it up for an easier and more rewarding pastime such as shooting a BB gun or riding a bike. Giving up did not appeal to me. I was what some of the old folks called "bull-headed." Once I started a project, I very rarely gave it up until I felt good about my performance. In my mind's eye, I could "see" myself throwing the knife accurately and dependably, just like the showman in a Barnum and Bailey Circus act. I believed I could do it. I knew it would take time and practice, but I enjoyed that part of the process, too. Even at that early age, I knew from experience and a deep-seated basic "feeling" that I could utilize this process and achieve the desired result, no matter what the project.

Usually for me, accomplishment of a goal, once it was set with all the required components, was just a natural process.

Although the system had not yet been formalized, once I decided I really wanted to do something and established a made-up mind, I began telling myself that I could and would do it, until I actually began to "see" myself doing it in my mind's eye. As I proceeded and learned from my activities—especially my failures—I would then make adaptations and corrections. Almost without exception, this procedure led to success. It was only when I yielded to the negative input of others or gave in to my own fears and misgivings that I would give up without putting forth my very best effort. And even in my childhood days, those times were rare.

Determined to master knife-throwing, for days on end I stared at the target, hurled the knife at it, and retrieved it for another throw. Through this sustained, loving pursuit of my goal, I soon began to innately sense a relationship with the knife. The knife was no longer a foreign piece of metal; it was as much a part of me as my hands and eyes. As the knife hurtled through the air, a part of my mental, spiritual, innate self went along with it, guiding it, encouraging it and praising it. Projecting my vision of perfection into the knife, I could feel myself controlling its rotation and trajectory all the way to the target. I loved the activity!

In that experience, I was able to transcend my "conscious self" and enter a more refined and peaceful state of consciousness that for years was to remain a mystery to me. This "other self" that emerged was guided more by innately "feeling" and "sensing" than by consciously "knowing."

Finally, when I came to be in total unison with the knife—physically, mentally and spiritually—it began to reach the target with uncanny accuracy. My playmates and others who witnessed this little kid throwing a knife like Tarzan were very impressed with my skill. Their approval was not the major

goal of my activity, however. Lost in the delights of performing this task well, I noticed that I was experiencing a great
sense of peace and joy—totally unhampered by conscious-
minded doubts, fears, frustrations, jealousies and other
distractions.

Once I achieved that feeling of oneness with the knife and
the act of throwing it, this feeling commanded my total attention and focused my mind inwardly. I was swept into this state
in much the same way that a leaf is drawn into a whirlpool.
The ecstasy produced by this mental and emotional transfor-
mation added a new dimension to my life. The physical,
mental and spiritual aspects of my personality were brought
together and focused into a single state of consciousness that
somehow I knew was not a part of me, but rather, an internal
force directing and controlling me.

As a child, of course, I had no conscious knowledge of the
dynamic metaphysical principles I was utilizing, or of what
impact this discovery might have on the rest of my life. I realize now, however, that I was beginning to learn how to be
inner-directed and to experience a working relationship with
my "Innate," or Innate Subconscious Mind. Guided by my
new-found Innate, the confusion, insecurities and fears generated by religious traumas during my earlier childhood began
to dissipate and be of less influence in my life.

The love for the knife from deep within me and the process
of throwing it produced a very pleasant, enjoyable state of consciousness that absorbed into the very fiber of my body and
mind. I wanted so much to throw that knife well that, with the
beginning of the birth of my "other self" and the process of
"being loved through," my old, conscious-minded self was
overwhelmed. Although I obviously was not sophisticated
enough to fully understand the complex processes that were

taking place within my mind, the discovery of the primitive principles involved in surrendering conscious-minded control of my thoughts, emotions and activities made this a wonderfully significant and memorable event in my life.

It seemed as though my body and mind now had combined to become an instrument of my inner self. I felt very calm, peaceful, whole and complete, united within myself— body, mind and spirit. I felt a harmony within myself and with my surroundings.

This is what some would call a transcendent state of being. I had stepped out of the materialistic, physical world and into the freedom of the inner world of spirit. I was being "thought through," controlled from within by some mysterious motivation, in much the same way that the needle of a compass is controlled by an unseen magnetic force. Although I did not fully comprehend what was happening, I instinctively knew that it felt right. It was an extremely satisfying experience that rewarded, encouraged and strengthened my persistency and focus at this very early age.

With that propitious event, I also learned the value of breaking a task down into its logically sequential elements and perfecting each one in its turn. What started out as a little boy's stubbornness became a very beneficial habit of persisting just for the sake of persisting, and I learned that my ability to be persistent increased with practice.

With my growing habit of determined persistence, I learned precisely how to stand, grasp the knife, swing my arm in the most effective arc and throw the knife with exactly the right thrust in relation to the distance to the target. My persistent Innate Subconscious mental influence also enhanced my ability to make the best follow-through weight shift to remain balanced and accurate. Almost before I knew what had happened, I had no competition for the honor of being the best knife-thrower in my neighborhood. I had paid the price to perfect this skill, and this "doing for the sake of doing," for the first time in my life, produced a great sense of inner peace. I could now throw a knife in a natural manner, in much the same way that accomplished musicians, dancers, actors, athletes and other accomplished performers might display their skills. Just as they do not have to consciously find the notes, count the steps, memorize lines or calculate the ball's speed, I, too, could throw my knife with an almost "mindlessly" euphoric and free expression of this internal and external skill. I have since learned that most exceptional performers are guided by this innate, inner ability that is often called "talent" or "instinctive ability."

You can learn the same principles that guide this ability right here, right now, as you read this book. The power is available to every living and willing individual. Believing intensely that you can will help put it in your mind's eye and keep it there.

Of course, as I said, I wasn't practicing my knife-throwing just to show off. Persistent practice of the new skill stimulated a newly discovered peace and joy that provided its own reinforcement. Just experiencing the directing influence of "Innate" in my life while performing the task well, knowing I had found a new dimension in my life that was not motivated by reactions to fear, was all the reward I needed.

Even at that tender age, in a natural, unsophisticated way, I was more interested in the esoteric mental and spiritual processes than I was in what the results of my activities might be. At school, I did not work just for gold stars on my test papers. I worked primarily for golden moments within my own mind. I would focus on what I wanted to achieve, seeing in my mind's eye and feeling in my body the reward of reaching that ecstatic level of perfection each time I went through the process. This was the primitive beginning of my "Lasting Purpose" philosophy, which has helped so many people reach their highest potential level of achievement.

In whatever I was doing, I wanted to remain in what I later called the "divine latitude." In this transcendent stage of consciousness, I remained thought-less while guarding myself, not allowing my mind to be attached to any divisive or negative emotion that sought to invade my mind. This state of consciousness could be continuously enjoyed once I mastered the required skill of ignoring various forms of distractive "mind chatter." As you will see in the pages ahead, this inner approach to life and its challenges led to honors in both high school and college as well as later achievements in business.

Using this strategy of remaining in the "divine latitude," while listening to my Innate Subconscious Mind as it provided the wisdom for achieving goals, I maintained high performance and scholastic achievement throughout my school life. It enabled me to rise through the Boy Scouts to the rank of Eagle, with several palm leaf awards after that. In high school ROTC, I was first made captain of the drill team and then the cadet colonel and commander of the school's senior regiment. I was also captain of the track, football and rifle teams during both my junior and senior years. Before graduating as an honor student and class orator, my classmates honored me by electing me president of the school's 800-member student body. I also enjoyed active membership in virtually every academic and social club on campus. Obviously, the system for achievement I was developing was effective.

I feel very fortunate that I established a working relationship with my inner innate self so early in life. Although I did not have a clear perspective of what was happening inside of me, such knowledge really wasn't necessary. For example, when I was 14 years old, my track coach had noticed I had a long stride and good speed, and he suggested that I train for participation in the 110-yard-high hurdles event. It was difficult for me to visualize the footwork and timing it took to allow me to clear one hurdle and then, in three strides, to successfully leap over the next one, continuing the process until the course was completed. Using common logic, I worked on the problem with my conscious mind for several weeks, but the model that I was using caused me to feel uncertain, awkward and unsynchronized. I was stumbling and falling on a regular basis and not performing well at all. It was very frustrating.

Finally, one morning long before sunup—and seemingly "out of the blue"—I was awakened by a thought flash as it pierced my conscious awareness. Immediately in my mind there unfolded the idea of a three-step sequence in which I would jump on the fourth step with my left foot. Even though I had not figured this out logically, I innately knew that this was what I needed to do to clear the hurdle without breaking my stride. I could see the process in my mind's eye.

In spite of my excitement, I was able to go back to sleep for an hour or so. When I woke up again, I was still certain that my dilemma had been resolved while I slept. I continued to see the solution in my mind's eye, just as though it were on a movie screen. I wrote the sequences down so I wouldn't forget them. When I got to school that day, I tried out what my "thought flash" had conveyed to me. The technique worked perfectly! I could clear the hurdles every time with a smooth, even gait. Of course, it took my muscle memory a little while to catch up, but my mind already knew exactly what to do and how to do it. I could see myself in my mind's eye clearing the hurdles cleanly and smoothly every time. I loved visualizing it almost as though it were real. With practice and my continuing adjustment to the guidance of my Innate Subconscious, in a very short time I was, as we say at Life College, "near perfect."

I thought about this somewhat mystical thought flash experience many times and tried to discuss it with a few of my friends. The negative reception given to my ideas, however, caused me to quit trying to share the esoteric experience. Other people were really not interested in what, to me, was very interesting since it was not something derived from my conscious mind by reasoning. Part of the reason could have been my inability to explain it clearly. Nevertheless, I was thrilled and very curious about this discovery and did not let a lack of philosophical maturity and insight hinder my going back to the source for more. I remained open and receptive to thought flashes—those inspirations and ideas that spring from your Innate Subconscious Mind.

In fact, I went on with the activities of my life with ever greater confidence, as this phenomenon continued to appear most of the time when I needed it. As a result, I just assumed that this was a natural process for everybody. I concluded that, in a way, it was just a natural function like my other senses. I know now that while everybody does, in fact, possess this "sixth sense," they are not always able to utilize it.

When you stand aside intentionally and let your "warrior within" speak to you through your Innate Subconscious Mind, you tap into a source of intelligence that is sometimes far beyond the ability of your conscious mind to even understand. Thought flashes, in effect, are from "the God within." It is possible to secure a steady stream of these communications to your conscious mind and establish a way of life that is very sublime and effortless. You can remain focused in "divine latitude," where the everyday living processes are calm, peaceful, compassionate and inspiring.

Helen Keller obviously was aware of the powers within her when she wrote in *Light in My Darkness,* "I believe that life is given us so that we may grow in love, and I believe that God is in me as the sun is in the color and fragrance of a flower— the Light in my darkness, the Voice in my silence."[1]

Simply being aware of this phenomenon without putting it into practice has very little effect on your life. Once you embrace it, however, and start living your life by its principles, the peace, joy and increased satisfaction with your life make the effort involved more than worthwhile. It is only when you are really able to claim it for yourself—to know the process and apply it to your daily life in a practical way—that it becomes of great personal value to you.

---

[1] Helen Keller, *Light in My Darkness,* ed. Ray Silverman (West Chester, Pa.: Swedenborg, 1994), 15.

I

Knowing That You Know

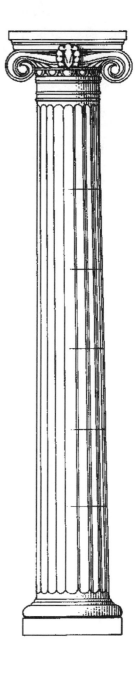

A LESSON LEARNED ON THE SCRIMMAGE LINE

My unlikely debut as a high school football player provides the best illustration of what a made-up mind fueled by desire and persistency—with the help of the Innate Subconscious Mind—can accomplish. The Innate Subconscious Mind is the part of your subconscious that generates verbalized thoughts and ideas. It is the source of our native intelligence, resourcefulness and creativity . . . and the root of my resolve to tackle the game of football.

I was already a junior in high school before I overcame my fear of physical contact and decided I was going to play this rough-and-tumble game, which, as you know, has the potential for causing serious physical injury. I still remember the commotion caused by my decision to try out for the team. My mother cried and begged me not to go. She told my friends, who had gathered at my house so that we could all go together to the first day of practice, that I was going to get my teeth knocked out. Some of the guys assured her that my teeth were perfectly safe, but she didn't believe them. (She was right, incidentally, because I eventually lost five of them!)

My mother's concern was understandable because not only was I her only living child, but I was also a young man without a lot of bulk on my frame. When I saw other bigger, heavier kids playing sandlot football and really roughing it up, that didn't appeal to me at all. I was somewhat shy and reluctant to join in when I thought about all those elbows and knees jamming into my ribs or having somebody's cleats come down on my face. Yet here I was, going out for the football team— and doing so with a no-retreat, made-up mind. This was not just a high school football team, either. There were only two big schools for boys in Atlanta at that time, and ours was a major team in the number one league in the South—and probably all of the United States.

Choosing to play at this level was a major challenge for me, and I learned what the power of decision and commitment was. All fear, which had previously held me back, left me. Still, I had little idea of what I was really getting into until I was selected to participate in my first scrimmage activities. The practice sessions had already been tough enough, being patterned after boot camp-type military training. These mental and physical challenges to my endurance proved to be like nursery school, however, compared with what was ahead of me. The ultimate test came when the coach challenged us to determine whether or not we personally had what it took to be football players in this demanding league with such a tough reputation.

A lot of the guys were able to be on the team just because they were big and strong. Many were very tough and had years of football experience behind them. Some of them really had exceptional talents, in addition to a lot of weight they could throw around. With my 139 pounds on a six-foot frame, I certainly didn't have size going for me when I weighed in on the first day of practice. Most of my competitors for a position on the team outweighed me by at least 20 to 30 pounds.

What I lacked in size, however, I more than compensated for with a deep inner desire to succeed, and with love, persistency and the ability to approach a task with a made-up mind. I recognize now that I was naturally talented and that talent was just looking for an opportunity to develop. I instinctively closed my thought processes to any "I can't" possibilities with this dynamic, positive belief that "I-can-if-any-man-can" attitude. Making use of this naturally bull-headed manner, I was driven by my Innate Subconscious Mind to put all my resources to work on any and all challenges I accepted.

As a result, I quickly began to acquire a knack for understanding my role as a football player. I was quick and fast and learned to carry out my blocking assignments with great precision—and with a sense of joy that often exploded into total euphoria. I looked forward to every football practice session because I loved the camaraderie and very much wanted the esteem, admiration and respect of the coaches.

The more I loved learning the playing skills, the better I got at them. And the better I got at them, the more I loved playing. I know now that on the football field that first day of scrimmage activities, I was practicing the Lasting Purpose principle of doing just for the sake of doing, with no ulterior motive in mind. By committing to the Lasting Purpose philosophy, I was helping to build the human resources of love and persistency.

When the coach first called on me to demonstrate my abilities, admittedly, I was shy and confused about the prospects of engaging in physical contact with larger, stronger and more experienced players while being observed, coached and mercilessly criticized. Scared or timid young men usually don't make good football players—especially 139-pound ones.

The first thing the coach did, which seems to be a common practice even today, was razz me with the vilest language a man could use. He then shoved me into position to be the "dummy" that's bashed around by the captain of the team. The captain was a very talented three-year football veteran who weighed in at well over 200 pounds. He had a large knot over one of his eyes that protruded from under his leather helmet and gave him a fierce look. I never thought of what he might want to do to me in order to maintain the esteem of the other players.

I awkwardly took up position to block this seasoned veteran. He was already in position, pompous, poised, professional and perfect in every way. Showing off to his teammates, he presented an admirable picture as he snorted and pawed at the ground with his cleats like a maddened bull. He could not have been more intimidating to me or more entertaining to his varsity teammates, and he knew it. Obviously, this was his purpose, and the crowd loved it. It was show time.

I came up to that imaginary scrimmage line and squatted, with my toes pointed out like a cub scout squatting around a campfire roasting marshmallows. With fear in my heart and guided by my conscious, educated mind, I assumed a stance wherein my shoulders were high and my rear end was almost on the ground—just the opposite of the way I had been taught during the first week of practice. When the coach jerked up his hat, as he had announced he would do to signal the start of the play, my rear end was no longer almost on the ground; it was quickly flat on the ground. The captain of the team had made his intended statement; he knocked me back with his quick 200-pound lunge as if I were nothing, and ran right over me. After hitting me square in the face with his elbows on his first charge, he stepped on my chest as I lay on the ground. He had meant to get my attention and entertain the audience of other players, and he did—in more ways than one.

When I got up off the ground, dizzy and confused, I straightened my helmet and tried to look at the crowd of players that had gathered around us. But I could not focus my eyes. I could see two or three images of everything, and the images kept revolving: going up and down, crossing and intersecting. When I was finally able to regain some of my composure, I noticed pain in my nose and around my eyes, which were beginning to swell and feel puffy. I could taste the blood coming from my injured gums and could see a lump rising on the bridge of my nose.

Before I could fully regain my composure and figure out what I was doing, the huge, square-jawed, 250-pound coach with steel-blue eyes and stubbled beard grabbed me by the jersey, put his face right up next to my rapidly swelling nose and eyeballed me dead center. At that moment, all I could see were two red-streaked, bulging eyes. I could also feel his huge, greasy nose and smell his rather remarkable breath. He didn't say anything at first. He just stood there, glaring at me, holding me in a face-to-face position. I remember he had these great big brown-stained teeth with wide gaps between them. The mouth then screamed at me: "Damn it, you little sonofabitch, didn't Ah tellya to block 'im? Didn't Ah tell you to spring out of yo' position and hit him first and hit him hard?"

"Yessuh!" I said.

"Then git yo' ass back down there and do what you were supposed to do!" he yelled. "Do you heah me now?"

"Yessuh!" I nervously blurted out again.

All the other ball players thought the whole episode was very, very funny. They were punching each other, pointing at me and snickering, eagerly awaiting the next act of the comedy. It was not one of my better moments, but my fighting spirit had been awakened. I could sense the difference in me, although no one else could.

Still fearful and searching my conscious mind for a solution to my dilemma, I assumed the same amateurish stance that had just gained me a whipping. In a matter of seconds, it was the same thing all over again. I was pushed backwards, laid out on the ground and beaten again. The crowd rolled in laughter and really got into it this time. The captain of the team obviously was enjoying himself as he strutted around like a game rooster, grinning from ear to ear, full of well-deserved pride over his dominance of the situation. The other players were getting their own kicks out of watching the captain's demonstration of his manhood, which, as I knew, was an important and healthy part of football. Once more, the coach sought to encourage me in his own inimitable way. Jumping around rather strangely while spewing a barrage of profanity, he loudly instructed me to "take off yo' damn helmet," which was still on sideways. I complied immediately. Then, totally without warning, he raised his hand high in the air and soundly impacted my skull with his huge University of Georgia football ring. The blow instantly produced a knot on my head about half an inch high. This totally unexpected, ritualistic blow to my head brought deafening laughter from the crowd when, with a dumbfounded expression, I began rubbing the bump with my hand. "You wanna play football for me, you little chicken shit?" he asked.

"Yessuh!" I stated emphatically, even though near to tears from the pain.

"Then git yo' little ass back down here and do it right, you heah?"

I'll have to give him his just dues. The coach did take the trouble to get down on the ground, place his feet properly and make a charge into my opponent to show me the exact procedure for blocking him. He showed me how to keep my rear end down, with my feet under my body and my shoulders level. He also showed me what I was doing wrong with my head and legs and how to get it right. He kept direct eye contact with me the whole time, as though he were controlling me with his eyes. I took in his every word, almost hypnotized by his stare. He definitely had my attention. The coach also had my total admiration, respect and love. I wanted his approval.

He was my leader and coach, and this was the way it was supposed to be. I allowed myself to be an extension of his will. I knew that if I did not exactly conform to his standards, it was his duty to find somebody else who would.

I realize now that when the coach hit me on the head with that ring, the pain of the blow distracted my conscious, educated mind. That allowed my ever-present and infinitely more intelligent Innate Subconscious Mind to take over. Suddenly, it was as though I were a totally different person. I was no longer reacting out of fear or embarrassment and thinking only with my sorely lacking conscious, educated mind. I had been transformed!

I was now very calm. In a flash, everything I had been taught the previous week came back to me just as though it were being fed to me by a computer: "Toes parallel, lean forward on your hands, then . . . head up and your shoulders square . . . lunge and charge and be first out . . . then drive, drive, drive, drive, always giving it your best effort the first time as though there would be no second chance . . . and never quitting until the whistle ends the play."

I felt the fear leaving my mind and body. I stopped trembling. I was no longer in the rabbit-like "escape and survive" mode. I could sense that, like an eagle, I was honed in for the attack—do or die. I had no thought of taking council with my fears or turning back. There is no doubt that my Innate Subconscious Mind was hard at work, giving me the message that would get me out of that embarrassing situation.

We did not wear a face mask or teeth guards at that time, but the potential condition of my nose and teeth didn't matter anymore anyway. "Something" had happened inside me when the coach's ring hit my head, and I instantly became very serious about the game I was learning. For the first time, I believed I could do what the coach had wanted me to do. I had undergone a definite and decisive paradigm shift. I was no longer making conscious-minded, fear-based decisions. My goal now was to block my opponent in a way that pleased the coach and me and that would also let my opponent know he had been blocked and blocked well.

Previously, I had been weak, indecisive and multi-purposed. I had had no resolve. I was just there—like a knot on a log. Now I was burning with desire, completely focused and ready to pay the price.

Although I had little in the way of a left-brain idea about the mechanics of what I was doing, I know now that I was about to unleash the power generated by a made-up mind (or mindset) to accomplish a single purpose. I was going to perform the techniques with a peak performance—no matter what! With the painful distraction provided by the coach's ring still pounding in my head, I immediately drifted into a kind of "dream world" in which I could see myself in my mind's eye doing what I should do and doing it right. With my inner eye—my mind's eye—in my imagination I saw my opponent being pushed back by my initial thrust and follow-through and then lying flat on his butt. And I believed it would happen just that way. I attached myself to that image like a stretched rubber band. I was there in my mind. I was no longer a stranger to my goal. The success was already mine. All I had to do was go through the physical motions that had allowed me to visualize. I was the victor.

As if by magic, I knew that watching the coach's hand was the key to being successful with this new challenge. I knew I needed to react the precise moment the coach tightened the muscles in his hand, right before he moved his cap to signal the start of the play. What I needed to do was anticipate the start and make my move the instant the hat began to move upward. Keeping my head up and looking straight ahead, I could still see the coach's hand well enough with my peripheral vision to react instantly. I knew that this extra split second would give me the advantage of initiating the contact with my opponent. I was not cheating by jumping at the moment the hand moved, but I was making sure that I moved exactly on time and not a millisecond later. I was not going to move after the snap, but with it.

I also knew that this very athletic football captain would be vulnerable to me only if I grabbed the advantage and hit him below his bruising elbows—down where the soft, defenseless underbelly began—and then drove upward with all my might underneath, up to and underneath his shoulder pads. It was also clear to me that if I came up from below him and sprang into action quickly, stopping him from charging and driving him backward through this surprise attack with rapid, piston-like movements of my legs, it would put him at such a disadvantage that in spite of my smaller size, I could overpower him. I saw this picture in its entirety in my mind's eye before the event occurred. I accepted it as an accomplished fact.

As I again lined up to take my turn at practice, while staring straight ahead at my opponent, out of the corners of my eyes I gave my full attention to the coach's hand holding the hat. As soon as I saw the tiny muscles of his hand move, before my opponent even knew what hit him, I smashed him, and the initial impact pushed him backward. The hat and I both moved at precisely the same moment. My mind, body and spirit worked automatically together as one. I hit him in exactly the right place, just as I had planned to do. I went straight under his elbows and shoulder pads into his belly, stopping him and driving him back, and my legs were like two pistons, driving rapidly with all the strength I had. This time, I could feel him giving ground and being pushed back! Then, all of a sudden, there I was, much to my embarrassment, on top of him after he tripped over his own feet. I had instinctively turned my action processes over to a different me—one that was focused and purposeful, one whose mind was made up. An unprecedented abundance of power surged through me. I kept my opponent going back for about five yards before he fell. He was incensed about being defeated by what he considered to be an unworthy opponent. He was like a young fighting bull that had made his first pass at the matador, only to find his horns full of air. For a few moments, he just stood there, brushing himself off and staring at me, unable to believe that this little Williams kid knocked him on his butt. Then this young bull of an athlete quickly got back down into position and started clawing and stomping, as though he couldn't wait for the coach to get me back in motion so he could repeat his earlier performance and again plow me into the ground.

This time, though, I was starting to get a little support from the crowd. And I'll always remember the coach's rapid change in attitude after I charged into the captain for the second time.

The coach now looked at me with obvious admiration, compassion and appreciation. He had a loving, affectionate, childlike smile as he said, "Boy-yie, Ah lak you!" All this time, younger members of the team were horsing around with one another and pointing at me in a sheepish, self-conscious manner, not wanting to offend our team leader. The assistant coaches had taken off their caps and were scratching their heads and shaking them in disbelief and admiration. They looked at me as though I were some visiting dignitary of royal descent. Little did they realize they were observing the birth of the real Sid Williams. In those moments, I experienced unprecedented focus, singleness of purpose, and the magic of believing and being directed by images produced in my mind's eye. Things have never been the same for me since that experience.

From then on, as the story of that exploit spread, almost everybody in the school seemed to know who Sid Williams was. It was a great time for me. I recall, however, that even though my status was greatly elevated, I did not indulge in self-pride and haughtiness. I was pleased with my achievement, but I knew it was not all mine. I knew I had discovered an entity inside me—the God within—that had made my change possible. I would not profane this innate power, this "warrior within," with vanity. My body was covered with chill bumps and tingled all over as I experienced a new relationship with my fellow students.

The smile and genuine expression of admiration by the coach still inspires me today and gives me strength in times of need. As the months and years rolled on, I came to have a great love and admiration for that coach. I would have done anything for him then—and still would even today if he were still living.

What was even more rewarding than that feeling of euphoria of the moment, however, was the lesson of life I had learned from the experience. As if by magic, I had learned to let my Innate Subconscious Mind act out the focused, concentrated images of my mind. I had had my first known experience of turning a problem over to the "warrior within," and the strategy had been wonderfully successful.

What I learned that day continues to influence my decisions and actions even now when dealing with challenges in every phase of my life. I used this internal skill throughout the remainder of high school and all the way through college at both Georgia Tech and the Palmer College of Chiropractic. I have also since applied it to every day of my professional career as a chiropractor, businessman, entrepreneur and educator at Life College.

Even today, the "dynamic essentials" that I utilize are the same, except for the strengthening of the influence of love and inspired belief, which I was to learn later in direct marketing.

If I had tucked my tail on the practice field that day and run and given up, it is unlikely that I would be writing this book today. Also, if I had tried to take on my formidable opponent "head on," "man to man," as my conscious mind wanted me to do, I would have lost the battle. Either way, it is possible that such an outcome would have tainted my self-image for the rest of my life. I may then have gone through life fearing failure, always seeing failure take place in my mind's eye, and having that negative image manifest itself repeatedly in my everyday experience. I may never have learned the value of being able to focus and to live in the "divine latitude," that peaceful state of mind in which love was my master, while sustaining an absolute belief in the vision of what I wanted to occur.

The only really hard part of learning to establish a correct mindset is developing the ability to believe that you can. You must let go of the rigid logical control dictated by conventional wisdom and allow your Innate Subconscious Mind to be master of your thoughts and actions. As it did with me, this insight is likely to come to you when you least expect it. I know now that the experience of that wonderful day on the high school practice field for me was the beginning of knowing that I knew. Follow the steps I will relate to you based on my personal experiences, and you, too, can begin the process of knowing that you know.

I CAN, I WILL, I MUST!

In 1947 I enrolled at Georgia Tech with a football scholarship I earned by virtue of my performance in high school playing two positions—quarterback and end. (I had also earned All-City and Georgia All-State Interscholastic Athletic Association honors.) Looking back now, I realize that giving myself to contact sports with such total abandon had to result in injuries. And they did come—much to the dismay of my coaches, my family and the insurance companies! Throughout my football career, I had seven bones fractured, three of them major.

Midway in my senior-year season in high school, I suffered a compound fracture of both bones in my right wrist and tore the cartilage in my right knee. The same year, on the very first day of practice at the Georgia All-Star game, I managed to acquire a serious fracture of my left collarbone, breaking it into three or four pieces. Because of the nature of these injuries, when I got to Georgia Tech the coaches must have thought they had a pretty poor bargain in me. I have no doubt they made some radical reassessments of my potential for participating in this high-impact sport.

Still, I never let the possible consequences of these serious injuries influence my courage, pride, or determination. I never lost my belief and confidence and never entertained the thought that I was too small or too fragile; quitting was never a consideration. As I sat in the stands week after week, still recovering from my injuries, most people thought that my chances of playing college ball were growing ever slimmer. But in the place in my mind where knowing really counts, I knew that with persistent effort, courage and painstaking preparation, I would one day earn the chance to play at the Division I NCAA level.

Among the many positive affirmations is one that, when spoken with authority, helps increase motivation and generate belief that the goal you're envisioning will be achieved. Affirm to yourself, with great inner force, that "I can, I will, I must," until you are able to say, "I am succeeding right now—this very minute!" These affirmations activate a faith and belief in yourself that will insulate you from any negative thoughts of quitting and, just as important, give you the ability to visualize your success. Even before I observed these inspiring words on the walls at Palmer College, I had already developed the ability to utilize these same sentiments, which would not accept my giving up in athletics or anything else, for that matter. I was locked in on the attributes of desire, persistent action, endurance, Lasting Purpose love and selflessness, which gave me an inward focus of the job I was doing as being already finished, and the results as I wanted them to be.

Although I did not fully understand what I was doing in my younger days or have the ability to use the principles consistently, I now know that each of my successes came when I continuously, persistently and with a strong desire spoke silently within myself and to myself with authority. With this method, I was able to instill in my own mind an absolute belief and visualization that allowed me to see myself in my mind's eye as a star player on the Georgia Tech team. All the circumstances and situations that tended to facilitate my football career came, I believe, as a direct response to the positive image I was able to generate in my mind's eye. Everything I have ever been able to achieve—often against what seemed to be insurmountable odds—can be attributed in one way or another to this ability to believe. As Napoleon Hill, the author of *Think and Grow Rich,* said repeatedly, "Whatever the mind of man can conceive and believe, it can achieve."

When I finally started practicing football again in the spring of 1948, I could tell by how the coaches avoided eye contact and ignored me that I was history as far as they were concerned. What they didn't say and do told me that I was already written off as being too small and fragile to be of any real value to them. This was especially obvious when I observed the high quality of the new players they had recruited.

If I was ever going to be discouraged, I had my best chance at it when I learned I had been assigned to the fourth-string varsity in the fall practice of '49. Almost everybody knew that assignment was almost as bad as being sent home! In those circumstances, I would never have been able to practice enough to establish myself as a player, either on the varsity or on the "B" team. I knew then that I would never play football at Tech except on the Red Shirt "B" team unless I could display my talent on a regular basis. I still had the mindset to be a top player and had established a made-up mind attitude that I would play. Being driven by intense desire and the silent, insistent affirmation of "I can, I will, I must!"—with, of course, the inner vision that this, in fact, was happening—the solution quickly came from inside my mind, and I fearlessly took precipitant action.

As solutions from the Innate Subconscious Mind often are, this one did not make a lot of sense to my friends, my parents—or even my more rational conscious mind. Nevertheless, I acted on it immediately. As directed by my "voice within," I went to Coach Dodd, the head football coach, the morning of the second day of practice and volunteered for the "B" team. This meant I would be subject to the same trauma and exposure to injury of 10 full games during the three-week scrimmage sessions planned to help prepare the varsity players for the tough 1949 SEC schedule.

Everybody in the football program was dumbfounded that I would leave the varsity and volunteer for the "B" team—even if I was assigned to the fourth string. Coach Dodd typically wanted what was best for his players and his team, but he seemed unconcerned about my request and routinely approved it. Looking back now, I'm sure he had already given up on me and had nothing to lose. He knew I would be good grist for his mill. As far as he was concerned, I was like a bird dog at a rabbit hunt.

It was taken for granted that nobody could survive the kind of brutality on an everyday basis that my kind of competitive play would generate. Consequently, the general consensus was that Sid Williams had been hit in the head once too often and was now trying to totally self-destruct. Nevertheless, I knew that I must prove to Coach Dodd and his staff that I was a player they couldn't ignore, so "damn the torpedoes, full speed ahead" I went.

Plowing into this challenge with unrelenting desire, belief, persistency, endurance and a made-up mind, coupled with love for the challenge before me, again brought successful outcomes. At the end of the first two weeks of practice, in a special segment of a highly emotional morning ceremony, my promotion to the varsity was tearfully cited by "B" team coach Roy McArthur to all his Red Dog team members as an example of what desire, courage, discipline and willingness to sacrifice could accomplish. Being the hard-nosed, demanding individual that he was, this kind of compliment from Coach McArthur was unprecedented. He told the members of the "B" team that Sid Williams' move up to the varsity team was an example of what all of them could do if they only had the intense desire and willingness to sacrifice. He explained to them that they all had the necessary talent or else they would not have received football scholarships at Georgia Tech. He spoke tearfully, saying, "Sid Williams has been promoted to the varsity today, and he'll never come back to the 'B' team! I promise you that. He has done what each of you can do if you only have his kind of determination to do it."

Needless to say, I went home that weekend filled with pride, relief and gratitude, and shared my joy with a very proud mother and father. I was promoted to second-team varsity in a single platoon system, which gave me virtual assurance that I would play most Saturdays with the Ramblin' Wrecks during the 1949 season. I was where I wanted to be and was supposed to be, with the opportunity to become a starter any moment.

From the beginning, I played the game with love, desire, focus, competitiveness and persistency. I had learned to rely upon my natural instincts and playing skills, which were always enhanced by painstaking preparation and visualization. I was not surprised when I was named as the starting defensive end in the early part of the 1950 season, when Coach Dodd went to the two-platoon system and the starting two-way end was injured. In fact, I was to retain the starting position of left defensive end through the 1952 season, ending in the Orange Bowl game against Baylor University in Florida, playing virtually all the defensive game time during those two seasons. The Georgia Tech defensive team in 1951 was ranked third in the nation by AP and UPI. It was great to be able to complete my playing days on one of Georgia Tech's greatest teams ever—the 1951 undefeated Southeastern Conference and 1952 Orange Bowl Champions.[1]

---

[1] I continued to watch my old team with pride as Georgia Tech won the 1953 Sugar Bowl in New Orleans and was voted NCAA Co-National Football Champions by the Associated Press.

Midway through the 1951 football season, Coach Dodd paid me one of his highest compliments ever in an article in *The Atlanta Journal* written by Edwin Pope, who later became the sports editor of the *Miami Herald.* The headline declared in the sports page, "SID WILLIAMS IS THE BEST END FOR HIS SIZE IN AMERICA."

Coach Dodd explained in the article what he meant by this statement. "He is very clever, moves well and hits as hard as any defensive end I have ever seen." As you might imagine, since I had overcome so much adversity, I was very pleased to have this College Football Hall of Fame coach, who was idolized by thousands of football fans, be so generous in his appraisal of my playing skills.

SPEAK TO YOURSELF WITH AUTHORITY

The next fortuitous lesson to have a lasting impact on my life came from my experiences with the Electrolux Corporation, the vacuum cleaner company, and the WearEver Company, a manufacturer of quality aluminum cooking utensils. After receiving my B.S. and finishing out the 1951-52 football season as a master's degree student in Labor Relations, I entered the business world, working for a local sporting goods firm in Atlanta. This proved to be only temporary, however, because I had a burning interest in chiropractic, the benefit of which I had first experienced during my stay at Georgia Tech. Then, in 1953, Dr. Nell and I were married, and on our honeymoon, entered the Palmer College of Chiropractic—the fountainhead of the profession. We quickly became two of the world's most outspoken advocates of chiropractic, and remain so today.

It was not until I moved to Iowa and started working my

way through Palmer that I was truly admitted to the "University of Hard Knocks" and received a genuine "graduate course" in achievement and in life. Although I had no idea of what was in store for me, I was soon to learn the true meaning of speaking to myself with authority, establishing a faith that could move mountains and living with love as my master.

Since we had to pay our own way while attending college, I looked for a part-time job that would leave enough time for my chiropractic studies. After assessing my marketable attributes, I knew that I had an outgoing personality, a neat, pleasant appearance, a ready smile and, of course, desire. I also had courage, not being at all shy now, and was a pretty good talker. As a rule, I liked people, and they usually liked me. I make this point because I knew that being a good direct-marketing salesman was far removed from being a mere "order taker" behind the counter in a department store, where customers usually come to the salesclerk with an interest in a particular product.

As I was considering what available product or service best suited my personality and abilities, I was encouraged by one of the field's leading direct salesmen to join the Electrolux Corporation's direct sales organization, even though I knew this endeavor would be tough from the start. I am glad I didn't give that temporary career choice a lot of serious preliminary thought because if I had, I probably would have passed it by. Many others had tried it and failed for a variety of reasons.

I especially wanted to discover the secret of selling myself and to be able to use this secret when I graduated as a chiropractor. I knew intuitively that I would have to be a great salesman to promote a health care profession whose educational institutions were not accredited at that time and that had been continuously declared "quackery" by the American Medical Association. The chiropractic profession was harassed almost daily by the media. So I knew instinctively that I could learn the "extra dimension" that I needed by talking to people who really didn't want to talk to me and selling them a product they really didn't want to buy. I was seeking personal training that would enhance my ability as a human being to persuade others to accept whatever products, services or ideas I might present, based on something inside me rather than only on customer interest and demand for the intrinsic value of the products themselves.

As I quickly learned, in order to earn a living with this new enterprise of vacuum sweeper sales, I would have to learn to get inside homes where I had no appointment and talk to people who didn't want or need to hear me. Then I would have to demonstrate a product that almost nobody wanted in the first place and had no extra money to buy even if they did! I found myself studying and training with salesmen who had the unique ability to persuade people to buy what they perhaps needed but really weren't shopping for. I admired these entrepreneurs and badly wanted to develop an ability like theirs so that I would have what it took to be a high-volume practitioner and a leader in my chosen profession.

Still holding onto the false pride and cowardice that faced me with this enterprise, unaware of how great a handicap this was, I prepared and rehearsed my sales presentation for weeks with great enthusiasm, until I had it refined to perfection. It appeared to me that there were no flaws. My understanding of the product was complete. I could answer any question that might be asked about it and parry any point of resistance with the skill of a musketeer swordsman. My enthusiasm was monumental, and I could see the tremendous potential that was there. I was emotionally prepared to sell vacuum cleaners door to door, if necessary . . . or so I thought!

In spite of all my meticulous preparation, I can now look back and see that I had been unable to speak with total authority, fearlessly complete within myself during my presentations with the vacuum cleaners. I always held something back. Either it was my respect for older people or my fear of stepping out alone and being an authority myself. Some major fear, which was highly unusual for me, kept holding me back. Therefore, I did not act as though what I told my prospects was the absolute truth and that they should act decisively on my suggestions toward purchasing the product. I did not speak with authority: that magic ingredient that generates belief. As I have discovered, when you repeat affirmations to yourself with just the right tone, timbre and cadence, the authority of your voice generates the belief in what you're saying.

The prospects were correct, therefore, when they were reluctant to act on my suggestions because they knew I was not fully committed as an authority within myself. That was clear from the tone of my voice, my behavior and my mannerisms. I instinctively knew that this was my weakness, and that if I could acquire this quality, it would help insure my success. Nevertheless, I would not fully commit myself. I was just dangling my toes in the water when I knew I needed to go ahead and jump in head first and either sink or swim.

With all these built-in handicaps, and without the required mental and emotional skills, it was very difficult, indeed, to find anyone who would simply volunteer to put out good hard cash for a down-payment on a vacuum cleaner—even an Electrolux, which had a reputation for being the best in the world at that time. Without the ability to believe and visualize my goal as being achieved, I was faced, instead, with a visualization of failure. I was being held back by my own deeply entrenched inhibitions, which prevented me from fully committing to my presentations with authority.

Even at that stage of my career, I knew that just having a positive mental attitude or being aggressive and talking loudly would not do the job. In most cases, in fact, that kind of superficial behavior just demonstrated to others who did know that I didn't know, and that I was really afraid.

As I was soon to learn, the real secret to consistent achievement is learning to speak to yourself with such absolute authority that not only do you believe what you are saying, but you are able to convince others as well. When you speak with total belief, people respond to you as an authority. Your own dynamic belief provides the spark needed to motivate others to help you achieve your vision. You can reach that state of belief by saying to yourself with complete authority: "I can achieve my goals. I will achieve my goals. I am achieving my goals right now. I have no doubts. I am achieving my goals right now, this very instant. I am successful. I am realizing my dream."

It may take a few days, a few years or a few decades for the reality you currently perceive to catch up with the reality within your own mind. Nevertheless, your unshakable belief, created by speaking to yourself with authority, sets into motion a vision of outcome potentials that can be produced by your new creative ability. The capacity to see the outcome of actual events in advance of others is what is commonly thought of as "vision." With the help of your Innate Subconscious Mind, today's vision can then become tomorrow's reality. When you hold this visualization in your inner creative eye, the ideas, people and other resources are arranged for you as if by magic in astounding ways that many may find hard to believe.

Regardless of how much talent I might have had, without this absolutely essential missing ingredient in my preparatory work, I was only ordinary at best and my efforts were doomed to failure, even though I had several assets in my favor. I could have been more aggressive, of course, and persisted with my foot in the door, but I figured this would only make people angrier than they already seemed to be. I had already had run-ins with several very determined dogs as well as some equally determined and hard-boiled housewives. Even though I did gain some very practical and potentially valuable sales experience from these temporary defeats, the only material gains that came from my vacuum cleaner demonstrations were more miles on my old car and thinner soles on my shoes. Little did I know at the time that my worn-out shoes would be playing a major role in the internal drama that was to unfold in the very near future.

Still somewhat bewildered by my initial lack of success, I desperately worked to convince myself that I had what it took to be a good salesman. This was very important to me because I occasionally doubted myself. I even rationalized that maybe I should try something else, lest this early sign of failure penetrate my consciousness. However, I remained like a piece of metal in a forge—ready to take the heat. This fortification of my mindset helped sustain me on my path to understanding.

Many potentially great athletes and salespeople give up in their minds long before they quit physically, so they never achieve what they're capable of achieving. As you will see as we proceed, the working principles of Lasting Purpose provide an ideal remedy for helping the "down-and-out" salesperson or any other discouraged person to get "back up and at 'em." With Lasting Purpose as a basic mindset, you continue to love, serve and give out of your own abundance, just for the sake of doing so, always building up internal love as well as your persistency. No matter what circumstances you are facing after using this procedure for a while, you are always able to love your work and, just as important, you are able to stay in the game.

Bruce Valentine—the person who was training me to sell vacuum cleaners—was in pursuit of a salesmanship award called the Diamond Silver Elephant Award. Even though he was a mild-spoken man who had trouble looking anybody in the eye, he had the magic formula for making sales. This amazed me because his approach was just the opposite of what I had always thought it should be. He had this very strange way of always looking between and just above the eyes of the person he was addressing and never directly into the customer's eyes. His voice was soft and genteel, but it had the magic to make people listen to him and then respond to what he was saying. I was awed by this man's technique. His ability to persuade others to do his will was uncanny. I wanted to be able to do it just like Mr. Valentine did it. His power humbled me as I bowed to his skills.

I placed vacuum sweepers in 12 homes for Mr. Valentine one Saturday morning just by having what they call in the trade the "dumb guts" to walk into houses where the screen door was unlatched, thereby enabling me to set the machines down on the living room floor. I usually was met by a distraught housewife pleading with me to please leave, protesting that she did not want to buy anything. And before I could excuse myself, this great salesman would walk in and start his pitch: "I am Bruce Valentine of the Electrolux Corporation. I have a machine to show you today." He said it with such love and authority that the housewife was immediately disarmed and overwhelmed.

As was routine in his procedure, the machine was immediately taken out of the box and plugged in. He was then asking the housewife with absolute authority, "Are you aware that household dirt contains nine disease-carrying bacteria?" With an alarmed expression of surprise, the women always said "No!" Without exception, the potential customers were shocked by this information and would then follow Mr. Valentine's every motion and word with the greatest of respect. (I remember trying out the same line on a cold-call customer early one evening, but she cursed me out big time while running me from her house and threatening to call the police to have me jailed for molestation.)

Moving along with his well-practiced, authoritative program, Mr. Valentine put a black cloth between the hose and the vacuum cleaner and began going over the bedding, chairs and sofas in the house. When he presented the black cloth to the housewife for observation and she saw that it was covered with a greasy, sinister-looking gray compound, he asked very sincerely, "Are you aware that you and your little children are putting your faces in this filth every day?"

As these women, often with their children hanging onto their dress, stood with their mouths open, shocked, Mr. Valentine continued, "If you could find a machine for as little as $10 per month that would eliminate this condition from your house, is that the kind of machine you would want?" Eleven out of 12 ladies responded that morning by nodding their heads, indicating that it was the kind of machine they wanted and they were ready and anxious to buy it right then and there. Mr. Valentine then took out his sales book, wrote up the order, and told them, while pointing to the appropriate line, "Put your name beside the X marked on this page." Without talking, he held them with his big eyes fixed on theirs. He then told them the down payment was 10, 15 or 20 dollars and asked which one was best for them. They all chose to pay $10 down and $15 per month, and went and got the cash from somewhere in the house.

What a master this man was! At that time, however, I still did not understand what he was doing and how he did it, and so I continued to hold back, unable to take immediate advantage of what my mentor had demonstrated. I could see what was happening before my eyes, but the essence of the process was not at all clear to me.

My previous achievements in life gave me every reason to be confident in myself. I was not a quitter. I knew there was an inner secret to direct marketing and that if I persisted, I would eventually know it. Still, I continued to be plagued by weakness, hesitancy and cowardice, and I lacked the inner courage and fortitude to speak to anyone with a made-up mind and then proclaim it with authority. I could not cut loose from my moorings.

I had only a vague notion about this phenomenon then, but I know for certain now that when you speak with authority to yourself it opens up the door to your Innate Subconscious Mind. That lets your spirituality unfold and you become a more likeable, more respected and more admired human being as a result. It also gives you a clarity of vision. When desire allows you to say, "I can, I will, I must," and you say it with authority, it creates the potential for belief in another part of your mind and confidence in whatever products, services or ideas you may have to offer. Because you then believe, you can see yourself accomplishing the goals you set for your mind. What you believe you can do and what you can see yourself doing in your mind's eye form a vision that begins to materialize.

Things you can persistently visualize can materialize if you persist long enough. If, however, you are visualizing with fear as your master and fear of failure as your constant companion, and if in your mind's eye you see that you will not succeed, you will be speeded in the direction of failure. If you believe you can, then you can, and you will be speeded to success.

Without being able to claim this great secret at that time, however, I was urged on by necessity and the desire to learn. So again I persisted and continued to make calls with little to show for my effort. At times, of course, I was tempted to quit and say, "What's the use? It really doesn't matter anyhow," especially when faced with only minimal, "barely surviving" success. Yet I continued to reject the thought of quitting. I was scarred and bleeding, but this did not break my faith. I was determined.

When my wife began demonstrating—and, more important, actually selling—WearEver cookware, I came to a logical "male chauvinist pig" conclusion that if she could do it, I could probably do it better. She made it look easy by selling two large $156 sets with her first demonstration. I knew that if a quiet, mild, warm, friendly person like my wife could sell two sets of cooking utensils so easily, then there was a strong possibility that an aggressive, loud-mouthed, warm, friendly person like myself could sell them by the hundreds.

There also seemed to be no limit to the number of potential customers for this product—especially the young working women who were passionately building their hope chests. People in those days could do without a vacuum cleaner and sweep their wooden, linoleum-covered floors with a dollar broom, but most women knew it took good pots and pans to cook a decent meal three times a day. Prospects for my new career looked good. I also knew that very few customers regretted making a purchase once they started using this fine product, so I could sell it in good conscience. Still searching for reasons outside for my previous failures, all the factors I cared to look at indicated that this was definitely the right change for me. I was desperate to find a dramatic solution to my problems so I would not be a quitter, and to stay in the sales game full blast.

Without hesitation, and with my usual enthusiasm and determination, I quickly launched into my new career as a WearEver cookware salesman. Just as I had envisioned, because I believed what the WearEver Company had told me, I found that with the help of a free gift, single working women could easily be talked into signing up for this wonderful product. With great enthusiasm, expertise and persistency, I set out to sign up as many as possible.

I was encouraged by several fairly quick sales. Very few of the young ladies who gave me the opportunity to make my pitch were a match for my persistency. As I later learned, however, many of them signed up primarily to get rid of me! More often than I care to remember, by the time the cookware was delivered, the "charming Sid Williams spell" had worn off and the majority of the young ladies refused to accept their merchandise. They had never really "bought" the product; they had been talked into signing an order against their will just to be pleasant and get rid of me. The big commissions I thought I had went down the drain. I was right back where I had started. This was not one of my better life experiences . . . but there were lessons to be learned from it.

I realize now that this second wave of disappointments came because I had not properly dealt with the first one. Instead of changing product lines when I did not produce sales, I should have had the courage to confront myself, take control of my mind and be courageous as I had been taught to be. Hindsight, of course, is always 20/20. At that time, it never occurred to me that possessing a strong desire and affirming in many ways that "I can, I will, I must" with authority was the magical key that would open most doors to which it was applied. Not even B.J. Palmer in his books had ever suggested that you should speak with authority to produce believability. However, as I have learned from much personal experience, when you speak to another part of your mind with absolute authority, it will believe. Your mind will acknowledge and respond positively to the authority it senses in your voice.

There are millions and millions of people who are trying to think positively and visualize positively, but they cannot do it because they don't believe they can do it. I had the good fortune of stumbling upon this concept accidentally by having a mind prepared to receive it. I soon recognized that a major revelation to me was represented in this new understanding. This process gave me the belief first and then the ability to create visions of successful sales encounters. Belief was the mystic key, and I had learned to increase my ability to believe. I then remembered what the Bible says: "All things are possible to him that believes" (Mark 9:23). In my own personal world, the discovery of this was revolutionary. It changed my perspective about achievement and success.

Still not fully appreciating the power of the discovery that was unfolding inside me, however, mile after mile I pounded on the steering wheel of my old car, chanting to myself over and over again for what seemed like hours: "I can, I will, I must! I can, I will, I must!" Overall, with the hope of strengthening my resolve, I must have repeated those words in some form thousands and even hundreds of thousands of times. Finally, in painful desperation, I pleaded to God to reveal the secret to me and not let me fail: "Please, God, give me strength to overcome this cowardice within me. Oh God, I am not a quitter. I am strong. I am powerful. I will not quit. Help me, God. Give me the strength I need. Please, God, keep this bitter pill of defeat from my mind and from my life. Please, God, keep me strong. I need your help, God. Don't let me quit. Let me be successful."

I hated both quitting and failure with a passion. My insistent and dominant mother had trained me well. I could not quit or do less than my very best, whatever the cost. I just kept persistently going on and on, repeating the affirmations ever stronger and stronger, and with strangely growing authority. The more I affirmed, and the more authoritative I got, and the clearer I sensed I was approaching my goal, I knew—somehow, some way—I would know that I knew.

At this time, I was still not able to see myself selling successfully. I could not believably say, "I am successful right now, this very instant—this very moment" because belief had not yet been realized in my mind, and I could not really see myself succeeding in the marketplace. Still, I could sense that I was on the right track and innately felt that very soon I could see the fields white with harvest.

Still relying heavily on my conscious mind, however, I tried desperately to figure out why it was that some were able to make sales that stuck while mine almost always fell through after they got cold. It just didn't make any sense by common, educated-mind standards that seemingly less able men and women would have more durable sales than mine. What were they doing that I wasn't? What was wrong with me?

Fear and hunger often give you renewed strength over trying situations and bring about great changes in your life, but nothing of significance was happening in mine as yet. Still, although these positive affirmations buoyed my confidence for short periods of time, only pride kept me from giving up. I continued to have that nagging, gnawing, frustrated feeling of incompleteness. I felt that something was about to happen inside me, however, because the flickering idea to give up grew weaker and weaker. The more I affirmed "I can, I will, I must!" with love and authority in my voice, the more energized I became. I would often smile at myself after a particularly long series of affirmations. I began to believe . . . a little bit.

PRESS HARD—THERE ARE THREE COPIES!

The turning point in my cookware sales career finally came one hot August day when a fellow student, Roy Mitchell, and I were calling on leads we had collected earlier. When making such one call, we were greeted at the door by a woman who declared immediately and emphatically that neither she nor her daughter, who stood beside her, needed any cookware or wanted to buy any. Since I was persistent, saying that a close friend of hers wanted her to see the product, I managed to persuade her to let us come inside. Getting inside, of course, was always an encouraging and necessary first step in making a sale.

I proceeded to give my finely-honed sales pitch, covering every aspect of the product and skillfully brushing aside each objection and excuse the lady presented. Still, she continued to resist, saying she didn't need any cooking utensils and, further, that she did not want any. Nor would her daughter loosen up. Desperate, but still operating on the assumption that the more I talked, the more successful I would be, I ate some more humble pie and continued my performance. I was determined to do whatever it took to make the sale. I had no intention of giving up.

The daughter's boyfriend came in about this time and he let it be known right away that he had other activities in mind to occupy the young lady's time and attention. Roy skillfully tried to divert the impatient young man's attention, and it quickly became obvious that this was not going to be an easy textbook closing!

In spite of all the obstacles, which already would have discouraged and run off most salesmen, I was being driven by an emotional momentum now that was carrying me forward with ease, and I wouldn't let up on the pressure. I'm not even sure I could have let up. This tiger had me by the tail. "I can, I will, I must" had been expanded to "I must get stronger. I can do this. I will do it. I will continue. I must! I must! I must!" These words kept echoing in the periphery of my mind, and I began deep within me at last, in another part of my mind, to believe the authority in my affirmations. I believed I was going to win this encounter. Fear of being offensive or being rejected were not a part of my cognitive processes. I saw myself in my mind's eye being recognized, appreciated, accepted and, more important at the moment, receiving that order. I could visualize the changes in the expressions on people's faces as they approved of me and accepted my direction.

I drove home the final point in my impeccable presentation. Using the company's "by-the-book" sales technique, I repeated the tried and proven leading question over and over again, and I was errorless: "If you were going to take these cooking utensils, would you prefer the large, medium or small set?" I would be very careful not to say anything that she could deny or say "no" to. If her mind started to go in the wrong direction, like a heat-seeking missile I would adapt and mentally stand in her way to redirect her thinking.

I was bulldoggedly determined not to get a negative answer

from this woman. I was going to have a "yes" in every sequence of the questions if it took all night to repeat the approach. As the power of my belief took over my mind, suddenly I stopped speaking. Absent-mindedly, I dropped down on one knee and reached for the sample one-and-one-half quart saucepan in my case that I always used in demonstration and that I was closest to. The image and emotions of that moment are as clear and satisfying now as if the event had occurred only yesterday. As I knelt down on the floor, leaning forward on my right foot to get the saucepan, the stitches in the leather sole of my right Cordovan shoe snapped, and my foot slipped out of the shoe and onto the rug. At that moment, the attention of my conscious, educated mind was totally distracted from the other events that were occurring in the room.[1] This distraction loosened my conscious mind's grip on what I was doing and, as I have said often, I wasn't "back yonder" and I wasn't "over yonder"; I was here in the present. I just was. This apparently released love that was in me naturally or had been generated in me (as it is in all human beings), and love was ready to dominate every aspect of my being. This love refers more to an attitude than an emotion. It enables you to reach out beyond any personal judgments you may have. By maintaining a mindset of love, you can always deal compassionately and effectively with other human beings.

Suddenly I perceived a hush in the room—a silence so

---

[1] I once read that evangelist Billy Graham also had such a serendipitous experience. With a very modest career at the time, he was playing golf one day when a falling leaf distracted him. As he watched the leaf spiraling to the ground, it reportedly occurred to him that he had not yet fully accepted the gospel of Jesus Christ in his own heart. Once he made the momentous decision to preach the Christian gospel in full faith and with complete authority, his ministry began to blossom. The rest of that story is history.

profound that it was an entity itself within me; it could not be ignored. I also noticed an attitude of reverence among those present in the room. No one moved or made a sound. I had the feeling that I was far apart from the mundane, physical event of the moment and had attained a oneness with love in the silence that had suddenly consumed me. My breathing was slow and very deliberate. It was so shallow at times that I was not sure for a few moments whether I was breathing at all. I found myself wondering if this experience was just a normal physical function or if my respiration was really a spiritual inspiration.

Up to that time, all I had wanted was a signature on the dotted line. I had been consciously pressing for the agreement with the customer and had been so forceful in my personality that I am sure I appeared close to being downright unfriendly. But now, as if by magic, my whole mood and demeanor changed. All the frustration, tension and anxiety that had been gripping me tightly just let go. I felt as if the world had turned me loose . . . or had I turned loose of the world? It was like the relief that comes when you take off hot clothes on a muggy day. In place of the frustrating stress and anxiety came a feeling of intense peace, tranquility and, of course, this profound, ecstatic, joyous inner feeling that was pulsating in the cells of my being. This feeling was continuous and multiplied itself like waves in a sea.

An unconditional love, a love for everything in the material world, totally consumed me. I was blown away in a thought-less love experience. With this resulting joy, I was transformed from a scratching, scrambling, fearful survival mode of being to a totally Innate-directed level of love-consciousness. This phenomenal experience is impossible to accurately communicate in words to another human being.

There have been some attempted descriptions of this degree of ecstasy by the very few human beings who are known to have experienced it, but they are rare.

I believe this was the same kind of transcendent experience that persistently devout religious leaders and prophets of various faiths throughout history have described as their spiritual experiences, which may have occurred once or twice in a lifetime. According to those who have written about this experience, the high point of the ecstasy usually comes with some great trauma, tragedy or profound meditational experience, typically only after months, years or even decades of praying, fasting and self-denial.

I have read of holy men, and have been in the presence of those who were in this state of ecstasy, whose educated minds and desires of the world had left them as they were captivated by a continual spiritual moment. They were in the world but not of the world. Spiritual centers on every continent have people like this—people who have removed themselves from society just to have this encounter. They have rejected all contact with the world and live a very Spartan lifestyle, subsisting on a simple vegetarian diet. These people are an instrument for this very spiritual and prayerful state. They obviously are happy in this ecstasy, but I question the value of such activities to the world at large. When I discovered the power of this kind of spiritual evolution, I chose to put the skill to practical use for the benefit of others. I, too, sometimes retreat to the purely spiritual, but, in the main, I choose to stay in the world but not be of the world.

I don't know how or why I was able to achieve this experience in the environment and in the manner that I did. I feel sure I had the ability all my life to have such an experience, but I am thankful I was finally able to discover it in myself at a relatively early age. It certainly serves to confirm the adage that "God works in mysterious ways."

Still immersed in love, I then looked down at that gorgeous, sleek, beautifully designed, shiny little aluminum alloy saucepan that I had carefully wrapped in the company-recommended soft, gray cloth. I cared intensely for it and still do today. That experience has colored my whole life. I can still visualize and bring back a strong memory of the event that is very satisfying. I can certainly bring back the humility I felt. Contemplating not the saucepan but the ecstasy of the moment can bring a longing for a return to that very special, humbling moment in my life.

In a continuously and rapidly developing state of euphoria, I began slowly, gently, and very deliberately to uncover the pan, and then held it tenderly, lovingly and respectfully in my hands. I regarded it with great affection and reverence because it was as precious to me as any object could be—as precious as a newborn baby is to its mother when she first receives it into her arms. I was completely out of my normal range of feelings and emotions. This was something different. My full attention was now being influenced by this "love experience" that had taken over my mind and body.

As strange as it may seem to the uninitiated observer, I was spellbound by this encounter. My relationship with this inanimate little saucepan continued to expand and dominate my emotions. Something very significant had occurred inside my mind. It was what some would call a paradigm shift of the highest magnitude. The fearful doubt, regret and frustration about my ability that had plagued me up to that time disappeared. All negative feelings and thoughts dissolved. I had intense concentration although I was very calm and peaceful.

I was totally consumed and humbled by love. It did not

matter that the object of my love was only an inanimate piece of molded metal. The all-consuming love that flowed through me from the inside out was not selective in its expression. The love in me seemed to fill the entire room, and it influenced all who were present. Their attitudes made a 180-degree turn, manifested by the smiles on their faces, their uninhibited, childlike movements and the close, careful attention they were now giving to my every action. Love dominated them and me, and this brought us together. Love was loving through me, enabling the huge abundance of *agape* love that comes from and through the Innate Subconscious Mind to express itself through me.

As though mesmerized, for a few moments I could not even speak, move my body or change my facial features, which had a surreal, detached feeling to them. I just held the object of my focused affection—the cooking utensil—lovingly and tenderly, and regarded it with an intensity of caring and closeness that was profoundly beyond the feelings that any previous relationship had ever produced.

Whether this very unconventional metaphysical experience lasted a few seconds or a few minutes I'm not sure, but eventually the silence was penetrated by a heavenly sweet voice singing praises of my product, culminating with, "Young man, I've been listening to your presentation and I want to tell you that I've always wanted some WearEver cookware. I have $20 I will give as a down payment. Can I have the middle-sized set?"

These words almost brought me to the point of tears, so great was my joy. As I eventually came to realize, I was being "thought through" and "loved through." My mind was controlled by love loving through me. I had not verbalized anything. The only communication was through my exhibition of my submission to love and caring for the cooking utensil. I continued holding the pan, putting the lid in place carefully and tenderly. I began slowly shining and caressing the pan with the gray cloth cover and regarding it with sublime admiration, as though it were a priceless gift or a treasured trophy from some esteemed royal personage.

As I basked in this blissful state of consciousness, with another, more temporal part of my mind I carefully filled out the required order form and then presented it to this sweetly smiling lady. Then, although still reluctant to even formulate audible words, I prepared my lips to speak to her in a soft, gentle voice. I was careful not to produce enough force to disturb contact with the love inside me, which I knew was very delicate, fragile and precious. I had already nervously asked all the questions required by the agreements in the contract, feeling almost unable to force my mind to attend to such mundane details. My whole being continued to express love as I casually and aloofly handed that dear lady a Number 2 pencil, pointed out the signature line and directed her to it with my transfixed eyes, saying, finally, "Press hard—there are three copies!"

While the effect on me of being consumed by love was enchanting, the effect on the people around me was even more interesting. The change in my prospect's demeanor was especially astounding. This particular woman had been extremely negative and even insulting at times, up to the moment of my personal metamorphosis. Now, as she took the pencil and began scribbling her name, she, too, seemed to have an inner glow. In fact, she had the appearance of being led by the same power of love that had been generated inside me and expressed by me. Then, even before I could get the order pad back from her, her daughter announced that she was interested in the large, $256 set! The mother quickly responded that she had $35 squirreled away in a sugar jar that she would give her daughter for a down payment.

Both the mother and her daughter then began giggling with the enthusiasm of children engaged in an exciting exploration. The daughter was so elated over the good news that she was getting her own set of cookware that she excitedly threw her arms around me. To my amazement and embarrassment, she squeezed her body against mine, exclaiming, "I just love it! I always wanted a set of WearEver cookware, too!" The way she lingered in the embrace demonstrated more than a physical motivation and, at that moment, it was obvious that she was excited about more than the cooking utensils. She was caught up in the same kind of mystical euphoria produced by such entertainers as Frank Sinatra, Elvis Presley and the Beatles, whose fans would scream and swoon in their presence. If her own behavior were not astounding enough, when I nervously glanced over at the previously hostile boyfriend, even he was now grinning from ear to ear, obviously caught up in the jubilation of that phenomenal event.

I continued to be humbled by the experience of love working in me, lifting me up in a natural high and carrying me along with it like a wildly cascading stream. After warm handshakes, serious eye contact and an exchange of pleasantries among all of us, we left the house. I was still basking in the delectable feeling of this new, totally consuming experience. Somehow, I knew that life for me would never be the same. I knew I had been lifted up to the top of the mountain and experienced heaven from that lofty perspective, even though I was still on earth and in a very physical form. I had reached a state of peace, bliss and love that exceeded anything I had ever encountered before in my life.

In those days, as was the custom of most men, I was a heavy

cigarette smoker—at least two packs per day. As I drove away, I started to light up a cigarette; but as I put it in my mouth and started to strike the match, I felt my new-found mindset of love begin to pull away from me. I sensed that if I went any further with this behavior, I would lose the contact with the love that was still within me. So I dropped the cigarette, put it back in my pocket and never had another thought about it. The destructive forces of a conscious thought associated with a negative habit were not compatible with the love that had consumed my mind. This love experience was very demanding and very jealous—not only concerning cigarettes, but about anything that required strong conscious concentration.

My tongue and lips seemed to be almost separated from my body and moved very slowly and deliberately when I tried to talk. It was a feeling somewhat like having my mouth anesthetized with Novocaine and beyond the control of my conscious mind. Being from the South, I had no trouble talking—almost like a ventriloquist—without moving my lips.

Although the physical me had a craving for a cigarette, another part of me was demanding that I continue to yield to the stronger power of the love within me. And I learned later that all other demands had to be second to love. The love I was experiencing was very jealous.

With the pack of cigarettes and the matches put away, I continued to surrender to the all-consuming expression of love that was bathing every cell of my body and mind. Love was directing my every move and even my thoughts and physical behavior. I wanted to continue this relationship with love as my master forever and ever. When you allow love to be your master, you do not allow attitudes or actions to interfere with your commitment to love, serve and give out of your own abundance. Everything about you is caring and compassionate, including your looks, your words and your mannerisms. Innately, I was motivated to do everything possible to avoid disturbing even for a moment this very fulfilling state of existence that had lifted me up, allowing me to experience this new dimension in life.

Humbled, yet eager to make another call and test the new me in the arena where it really counted, I asked Roy if he had any more leads we could call on. Roy told me the only other lead he had was, in his opinion, a very poor one. The lady was a single working woman in her thirties who lived near the Rock Island Lines railroad tracks and who was not likely to be building a hope chest.

"Let's give it a try, anyhow," I said, barely able to articulate the words, still mesmerized by this "inner world" feeling that had overwhelmed me.

It was not long before we arrived at a gray-weathered, unpainted house just a short distance from the railroad tracks. After taking a deep, satisfying breath, I walked ahead with confidence, carrying only the sales book and the saucepan that continued to be the object of my love. And I held it lovingly and close to me in a thought-less, yet precise, caring manner. Roy was close behind with the sample case as I approached the woman. No longer guided by insincere, emotionless memorized openers, I greeted this dear lady with all the love of my being. I let the love express itself through me fully.

Wearing a homemade feedsack dress, which was the common fashion for that area of rural Illinois and that time of week, our chosen prospect was busy hanging out some other simple clothes on a line in her back yard. At first, the lady was very unreceptive to my presentation, declaring emphatically in her crisp Midwestern accent that she was definitely "not interested in buying no cookware." With love as my master, which was reflected in my voice and already expressing the love that would bind us together, with complete honesty and sincerity, I implored her to "please help a poor Palmer student working his way through college." She remained unimpressed and came close to being insulting several times, but the aura of love being projected to her through me would not allow that degree of hostility to build in her. I stood there, without thought, and let the expression continue to guide me and produce the euphoria within me. She was as stubborn as a billy goat, but the love in me respected her for this. Nothing could deter me. As I recalled the very uplifting and satisfying love experience of the previous demonstration, I was inspired to believe she would let me show the product.

Then, with my whole demeanor ruled by love, I entered into Phase Two and explained to the lady that I was paid to show the product whether she bought anything or not. When I showed her the free gift, an aluminum pie pan, she grudgingly relented and led us through the back door, through the kitchen and then through the living room.

As we passed through the living room, we were greeted by both the sight and smell of a very drunk man sleeping on piles of dirty clothes on the couch. The floor was bare and had holes large enough that we could see the junk and trash piled beneath the house. I wondered, with some concern, what kinds of critters made their home with this lady after the lights went out at night.

We were led out to the front porch, where Roy claimed a seat on the steps. With total confidence and with very slow, deliberate, careful moves, I perched on my sample case, continuing to exude love for that one-and-one-half-quart saucepan that I held tenderly in my hands, wrapped, as usual, in the company-recommended gray cloth. I continued to be overwhelmed by the feelings that welled up inside me and was nearly in tears as I again looked at and touched the saucepan. I was instantly consumed and possessed by the same delicate, caring feeling of oneness with that little saucepan as the joy within me released itself.

I knew I was still in this world, but I felt I definitely had been transformed in some mystical, ethereal manner. I felt that not only could I reach out and touch a star, but that I was a part of each and every star. We were all a part of the same cosmic soup that stretched both outward and inward into infinity. I had a spiritual perception of all life. I remembered the book by Albert Schweitzer in which he talked about the kinship of all life and, in that moment, I understood what he meant. My conscious mind, emotions and will were no longer dominant in my life. I continued to be controlled by the love that flowed through me.

This experience was so intense, delicate and sensitive that, as earlier, I found myself barely able to articulate words without yielding to tears of joy. I also discovered that to retain this euphoric, transcendent state, I had to avoid utilizing my conscious, educated mind to reason. Making decisions was very difficult. If I became too attentive or too forceful, the feeling of captivation seemed to pale and fade. It was as though the lights were being turned out with a rheostat. I could very delicately sense the enchanting feeling loosen its grip on me as I deviated. The ethereal feeling seemed to glide away from me and the full impact of the outpouring of love could no longer be perceived. The encounter was very fragile and delicate, like listening to a very distant radio station that tends to fade out with the slightest interference.

I found that by diverting my attention to the pan again and totally surrendering myself to the love feeling, I would continue to be lifted to new heights in a distinct, unworldly manner that served to free me from either the positive or negative influences of the physical world. As I recalled from the Ten Commandments that "I shall have no other gods before me," I wondered if this was the same phenomenon. I had learned that when I was seeking to achieve this sublime state of consciousness in which love was my master, love itself was extremely jealous and permitted no conflicting mindsets, emotions, thoughts or behaviors.

Before I could utter more than five words of my greatly cut-down prepared talk, my innate connection with the prospect was firmly established. We were together as one in spirit. I was amazed to hear this resistant prospect announce from her broken straight-backed chair, "Well, to be quite frank with you, I've always wanted a set of WearEver cookware, but I never could decide to buy any, and I'm so thankful you are here!"

Once again, I was pushed along like a leaf in a stream as I gently and lovingly let the words pass from my lips, not really thinking, but more or less opening up to allow an outflow to begin. First, I thanked her very caringly, warmly touching her on the hand as I passed the saucepan to her. "If you were going to get a set of WearEver," I then asked, "which would you choose—the small, middle-size, or large set?" As I believed she would, she immediately responded, "Oh, I prefer the middle-size set, and I do love it, and, furthermore, I would like to buy it. Would $20 be enough for a down payment?"

I was careful to play the game by the book and not take the customer's response for granted. I was not going to gamble. Even though I had reached a new height in sales work and in life itself, I was still careful to use the proven approach that guaranteed a successful outcome. I mumbled an answer that seemed to come from another dimension. "Yes, it would be,"

I replied, struggling to form the words with my reluctant tongue, the sounds creeping out in a low, guttural tone. Making out the order form and continuing with love as my master, I passed the book and pencil to her. As with the prospect before her, she now seemed transfixed. She looked me in the eye, almost seductively, for further directions, and I pointed to the "X" I had marked on the order form for her signature. I then told her very deliberately and reverently, with inner-directed low tones, "Press hard—there are three copies!"

I watched with awe as the pencil scribbled out her signature. She then clapped her hands several times with joy, wiggled almost sensually in the chair, and laughingly—almost coquettishly—exchanged glances with both Roy and me. There very definitely was a sensual component to her mood of the moment.

As I was leaving from that second call, we shook hands and exchanged deep, knowing glances several times. As a special gift from me to her, I gave her three of the sample saucepans and asked if she could give us the names of some of her friends who might be building a hope chest. She laughingly said, "I'm not building a hope chest, myself. My hope is that I can learn to cook a good meal, and I'm glad you came along when you did. This will give me a good start."

I again was humbled and made keenly aware that something new and very special was at work in me. I was changed in a number of significant ways. I realized that what was now working inside me had never consciously driven me before. I felt its wisdom and its power and recognized it as something rare yet precious, rewarding, satisfying, joyous and fulfilling to me. I also felt it was something that, if nurtured and respected and its process of achievement reduced to a habit, would be a great asset in my life as well as inspiring and comforting to others. Over the years, that expectation has continued to be confirmed on a daily basis.

For the next several years, I remained completely consumed by this intimate "love experience" with that cooking utensil. During this time, I was actually existing in a kind of "heaven on earth," with no thoughts that were not based in and directed by love. As I was being loved through, I was able to share this love with all activities, all things and all people I encountered. I became an extremely poor student at Palmer College of Chiropractic, of course, going from close to a 4.0 average to near failing. Nevertheless, as a cookware salesman I was now "neeeeear perfect"!

YES, YOU CAN

To achieve, believe; to believe, speak to yourself with absolute authority. Simple affirmations, as they typically are used, have little lasting value. It is only when you learn to talk to yourself with absolute authority that you are able to believe what you are saying. Once your own mind believes what you are saying and accepts it as fact, that belief, in turn, produces a clear vision of what you want to achieve. That vision, then, is like a magic magnet that attracts the ideas, the people and the other resources needed to turn your vision into reality. That, in short, is the formula for success that I have found to be without equal.

There is no way that I can describe exactly for you what an authoritative voice is; nevertheless, when you perfect it, you'll know because you'll start believing what you're saying to yourself, and the vision of success will appear in your own mind's eye. Using just the right tone, just the right timbre, just the right meter and just the right cadence, you talk to yourself with absolute and irresistible authority, saying, in your own words, as appropriate for the task at hand, "I can achieve this goal! I will endure! I will persist! Nothing can stop me! Whatever it takes to do this, I'll make the sacrifice! I'll pay the price! I will overcome all obstacles! If I can't go through it, I'll go around. If I can't go around, I'll go over it. Even if I'm beaten and bloodied, I'll stand up to the challenge!"

Using your conscious mind, you utilize the authoritatively spoken affirmations that are needed to guide yourself in the direction you need to go to be effective. Whatever you affirm, you say it with such depth, such feeling, such emotion and such total sincerity that the other part of your mind cannot help but accept and firmly believe what you are saying. That is the crux of this whole system. The quality of what you say must be such that it would be believable by anybody if you were talking to someone other than yourself.

You must talk to yourself in the same manner that Winston Churchill and Franklin D. Roosevelt talked to the people of the United Kingdom and the United States, respectively, to lead them to victory in a world war that in the beginning seemed hopeless for the Allies. As President Roosevelt so famously said, "The only thing we have to fear is fear itself."

With any great enterprise, somebody is always saying, "You can't do that," "You're not smart enough," or—most painful of all—"Who do you think you are?" You are at war with fear and self-doubt as well as with the negativity of others. To be successful, you must be able to respond to your own self-doubt as well as that of others with absolute, incontestable authority, "I am! I am capable. I am capable right now, this instant, and I will do it. I am deserving. I will have it. I am doing it!"

When you speak to yourself this way with incontestable authority and start "acting as if" with equal authority, and when you accept the authority of what you are saying and doing, that's when you begin to believe. Then you have the ability to visualize what you want to do. Until you believe you can, you really believe you can't—and that's what gets you into trouble. When you believe you will fail, you usually do.

But once you develop the skill of talking to yourself in a way that is completely believable, a bit of magic begins to take place. In another part of your mind, you start firmly believing that you can and will achieve your goal. You tell yourself, "I have the desire to do this. I have the intelligence and skills to do it. I have the training. I have the persistence to do it. I can do it. I will do it. I can see in my mind's eye that I am doing it. I'm doing it right now—this very moment!"

When you are able to talk to yourself in this manner with absolute authority, your voice resonating credibility, the image begins to appear in your mind's eye—the inner eye, the creative eye, the eye of divine love, wisdom and justice. At that point, you just automatically begin "acting as if" your goal is already achieved. In your mind's eye, you see the deed already done: You have your degree, you have your complex built, you have your book written, or whatever it is you want to achieve. Then, keeping that visualization fresh and strong in your inner eye, you just let your mind flow backward from that image of success as you complete the steps required to get there in the world outside your own mind.

Once you're there in your mind's eye, your Innate Subconscious Mind will begin to help provide the people, ideas and resources needed to achieve your purpose. This doesn't mean you just concentrate on a picture of the future, spending all your time wishing you were there. When you truly believe you can, you continue to "act as if" it has already happened; you continue talking to yourself with absolute authority and believing with all your heart that what you see in your inner eye has occurred. With time and persistency, it will. The first step toward establishing an achievement mindset, of course, is to learn to love, serve and give out of your own abundance, just for the sake of doing it and for no other reason. You learn to love whatever you're doing, whether it's digging a ditch or adjusting a subluxation, and you learn to carry that love with you. This habit builds up your abundance of both love and persistency.

With a Lasting Purpose mindset to love, serve and give, you can be successful and make a living at any occupation you really desire to be successful at pursuing. Whether you are a homeless boy in Brazil or a farm girl in the U.S., you can be a doctor, a lawyer, a millionaire entrepreneur, a scientist, a ballerina, a writer or anything you have a burning desire to be.

You can find a great abundance of success legends in every country in the world, and a major ingredient in every one of those heroic stories is belief. What I am telling you here is something you are not likely to learn anywhere else, and that is how to achieve the belief that will produce a vision and, ultimately, success. Once you maximize your desire and lock onto your goal with a made-up mind to achieve it, telling yourself with absolute authority, "I can do it" and "I will do it" until you firmly believe that you can, the ability to visualize will be developed. Then, in most cases, what you can visualize will become your reality. To borrow from Napoleon Hill again, what the mind of humans can conceive and believe, the mind of humans can achieve.

Some people spend their whole lives lamenting their inherited lot in life. They compare themselves with others who are born with all the advantages of wealth and social position and use the perceived "unfairness of it all" as an excuse for lethargy, dishonesty and failure. Many people from humble beginnings, however, use their burning desire, willingness to sacrifice and belief that they can achieve their goals to reach the top of virtually every vocation and enterprise that exist. Rather than complaining about what they have been dealt in life, they maximize their assets and concentrate on achievement in the one area where they are most talented. They believe they can succeed, and then the automatic process begins to unfold.

You can lose a poker game with a full house, and you can win it with a pair of deuces. Winning or losing is not determined by what cards you are dealt in life, but how you play those cards. You don't have to be born rich, good-looking, athletic or super intelligent to be successful. If you are able to speak to yourself with such great strength and authority that you ultimately firmly believe what you are saying, then even if you are the fabled "ugly toad," you can still achieve in the manner of the "handsome prince." The "magic kiss" that makes the difference is belief. When you are able to say to yourself with complete authority, "I am a handsome prince," you will cease to be the ugly toad. You will be what you believe you are.

If you never had a real desire to achieve, or if your desire has been snuffed out by your own negativism or that of others, half-hearted affirmations of "I can" and "I will" are not very good crutches to get you going. Effective affirmations are more the result of your desire and your treasured vision than the cause of them. When your desire is so great that you cannot imagine your life without achieving what you desire, and you are then able to speak to yourself with such great strength and authority that you firmly believe your affirmations, then your Innate begins to tell you that you can and will do it.

Very few people in the world have a "natural talent" for success. Whether it's hitting a home run, making a perfect golf shot or belting out a song, the ability to make a performance look "easy" usually comes only after years of hard work and many failures. If you listen to the success stories of most of today's top entertainers, you will learn that nearly very one of them was scared to death when they first walked out on a stage or in front of a camera. These people continue to get over their initial stage fright by just doing what they need to do. Confident of their talents, they know they can do it. Then, with a made-up mind fueled by a burning desire, they tell themselves with absolute authority that they will do it. Even before the first applause, they know they have succeeded. They can see it, hear it and feel it. Whether they are consciously aware of it or not, the thought comes to mind, telling them, "I am doing it. And I'm doing it right!"

The affirmation of "I must" typically is not used unless you feel yourself weakening in your resolve. In fact, "I must!" often is a cry of desperation. Sometimes when you see yourself slipping and fear of failure starts creeping in, then you start thinking, "I can't fail. It will mean the end of my world. I've got to achieve this. I must do it." Sometimes "I must" is a sign of weakness that comes from the fear-based thoughts of "I didn't need to do this, anyhow. I don't have the strength to risk this failure. I don't want to make this sacrifice," or "I really don't deserve this success."

"I must" is used in the same way that you shift down to a lower gear when you feel your overloaded vehicle starting to choke on a hill. It's blowing on the embers and throwing on more wood when your fire is about to go out. When you desperately cry out to yourself, "I must do this," you are signaling that your motivation, your confidence and your enthusiasm are getting low. You're beginning to feel that you're losing heart or that the opportunities have passed you by, and you're almost ready to throw in the towel.

Everybody gets down sometimes, but when you feel one knee touch the ground, that's the time to shout to yourself with resounding authority, "No! I won't give up. I must get up. I must succeed." And in most cases, your strength will return. You will get up, you will relight your torch . . . and you will succeed.

Love is the fire that feeds your spirit and keeps you going when every other part of you wants to stop and give up. When I was trying to train myself to be a top achiever in the direct sales business, I needed all the help I could get. So with great desire and great persistency, I began to speak to myself with absolute authority, repeating over and over, "I can do it! I can do it! I have the ability. I have the desire. I will achieve this. I will endure. I will not quit. I will not surrender. Whatever it takes, I will pay the price. I can do it." And then when I felt fear begin to creep into my mind, I simply increased the intensity of my affirmations: "I must do it. I must not fail. I must persist. I must endure." As I continued to increase the momentum of my chanting and my enthusiasm continued to build, the first thing I knew, I started believing I would be successful. I not only *would* be, I *was!* So then I began saying hundreds of times, "I am success!" I continued to repeat this affirmation rhythmically and with great authority, depth and fervor. I would be nearly celebrating at this point. I could feel it and see it because I believed it.

These affirmations helped me over the obstacles of doubt and discouragement and reaffirmed my confidence in myself and what I was doing. They helped provide a mindset that allowed me to be open to experiencing and understanding the love phenomenon that occurred with that little aluminum saucepan.

Very few people will ever experience the "heaven on earth" that such an all-consuming love can provide. Still, by learning to practice loving, serving and giving in your everyday life, and by being persistent in whatever you do just for the sake of being persistent, you will have a great advantage over most other people when challenges and opportunities present themselves. You will always have love and you will always have persistency. Those two ingredients are like wild cards that you can use to enhance any hand that fate chooses to deal you. Whether rich or poor, in possession of one talent or 10, blue-blooded or hot-blooded, you can still be a competitor. And you can win!

2

Learning to Live with Lasting Purpose

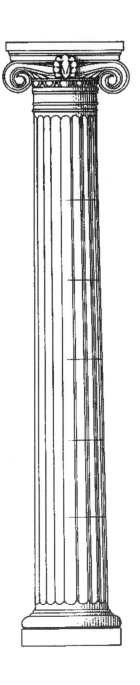

THE MINDSET OF LASTING PURPOSE

You have now learned from my experiences the value of knowing how to talk to yourself with authority and how to initiate the landslide of activities that can result in a firm belief in the affirmations you repeat to yourself. You have seen how this results in the formation of a credible vision in your mind's eye and, finally, in absolute belief in that vision in another part of your mind. You also have seen how this absolute belief triggers the confidence in yourself that allows you to say, "I am!"

I invite you now to use this system for developing a mindset—a totally focused, made-up mind—to incorporate Lasting Purpose as a major part of your daily life. Cultivating this mindset is crucial to the overall philosophy of Lasting Purpose. It indicates an irreversible decision on your part to proceed in a certain direction. Whether you are playing football, selling cookware or pursuing Lasting Purpose, having a mindset for achievement is essential to success.

The first step is to repeat to yourself with total authority the affirmations required to establish a Lasting Purpose mindset. You might say, "I love my work. I love my association with people. I love the product that I'm selling. And I am loving these things just for the sake of loving. I am working to achieve the task before me just for the sake of achievement. I am persisting in all that I set out to do. I am building up my abundance of love and persistency. I am loving. I am serving. I am giving. I love to love, serve and give out of my own abundance. I am allowing love to love through me. Loving makes me feel peaceful and joyful." Here, too, as you build up the cadence of your affirmations and build up your enthusiasm, always speaking with total authority, eventually you will be able to say, "I am living the Lasting Purpose life. I am love. I do not have to reach out and find love. Love is loving through me right now, this moment." Your vision will be a reality.

It's important to realize that you and I and everybody else have the freedom to choose a major mindset, such as Lasting Purpose, as well as all the various attitudes through which we see and interpret our world. Whereas one person may see a particular situation as an unbearable burden, another may see it as a wonderful opportunity. One person's hell often is another person's heaven. It all depends upon the mindset you choose. With your daily endeavors guided by an innate understanding of a Lasting Purpose mindset, which is motivated by the deep and earnest desire to love, serve and give out of your own abundance, each day's journey through life can be a productive and enriching joy—a true "heaven on earth."

With a Lasting Purpose mindset, you are freely and joyfully giving to others such wonderfully compassionate and valuable gifts as praise, encouragement, confidence, helpfulness, guidance, cheerfulness, leadership, forgiveness, a positive direction, respect, admiration and a positive self-image. As you give of yourself in this manner, your internal abundance of love will multiply and then be sustained during more trying times by the memories of love, friendships, appreciation and joyous moments created for others as a result of your giving. The more you give of yourself in a Lasting Purpose manner, the stronger you are, and the more love you have, the more spiritual you become as you build your life upon a firm foundation of love.

Finally, at the right moment, if it is your earnest desire to have it do so and if you have developed the ability to talk to yourself with authority, love will completely fill your life. I am not talking about just the feeling of love. I am talking about the powerfully solid entity of overwhelming, spiritual *agape* love, which can then become your master and love through you.

The difference between Lasting Purpose love and the kind of love experienced by most people in their lives can be understood with this example: If you wanted to preserve a board for outdoor use, you could buy a preservative solution and paint it on the post and it would do a pretty good job. If you really wanted your post to last, however, you would get one that was pressure-treated at the factory so that the preservative is forced into every fiber of the wood. That's the way Lasting Purpose love works. It is "forced" into every fiber of your being, so it affects everything that you think, say and do.

When you conduct your life in this boldly loving manner, each day's journey, no matter where it may take you physically or what positive or negative events may be taking place, will bring you joy. Joy is yours because you are giving just for the sake of giving and always reaping the great treasure of love that is building up within you. And as you also build up persistency, your potential for achievement has no limits.

Aristotle taught that the formation of good habits was the basis of moral excellence. Making Lasting Purpose a habit can add an almost mystical element of wisdom and power to your daily life. It acts as a catalyst, with a drive of its own to attract and organize whatever resources you may require to set and achieve progressive goals, and to make positive achievement a comfortable habit.

Lasting Purpose provides you with a time-tested, practical philosophy of life to help you become and remain a healthy, happy, productive and achieving individual—whether your natural assets and talents are great or ordinary. If you have no philosophy to guide you, it gives you one with great utilitarian value. If your philosophy is weak and shifting, Lasting Purpose can test it and firm it up for you, throwing out that which is of no value and strengthening that which can help you along your way.

In a sense, a Lasting Purpose mindset is like a loosely woven basket in which you can carry all your ideas, your emotions, your attitudes, your goals and your dreams. Those thoughts and activities that are incompatible with Lasting Purpose tend to fall through the basket's cracks, while those that support Lasting Purpose are strengthened and augmented.

Lasting Purpose also serves as a lighthouse of wisdom to guide you in your daily life, keeping you in the center of the channel of a love-directed life and away from the rocky reefs of hate and fear.

There are some people who live their whole lives with a Lasting Purpose mindset guiding them to love, serve and give out of their own abundance, and they're only vaguely aware of the phenomenal principles that guide their lives. They simply had the good fortune to find themselves in the right environment and with the right mental and emotional equipment to develop a natural, loving mindset. Once they learn to operate that way, they don't want to be any other way. These are the people who are consistently loving, enthusiastic, helpful, supportive, encouraging, always full of energy and always there with a kind word. They skirt around negative situations and parry hostile remarks with positive, productive alternatives.

People committed to letting love be their master are liked and respected by just about everybody they meet. As a result, most people want to help them accomplish their goals and objectives, which makes it easier for them to be achieving, successful individuals. These are the people you want to seek out and from whom you want to learn. They are the people who can not only help you enhance your own life, but who are eager to do so.

Of course, I do not expect everybody who reads this book to go out and make great achievements that reshape the world. It's possible that a few readers will have the special ability and the God-given inspiration to do that. For most people, however, the real value of Lasting Purpose is that it allows you to be happy and at peace with yourself and the world in whatever circumstances you may find yourself. With a Lasting Purpose commitment to love, serve and give out of your own abundance, you can be farming, driving a truck, teaching school, running a small business or managing a home, and find your life very rewarding. You don't have to be at the top of the mountain to experience heaven in your own mind.

Many people at the top of their respective professions are miserable. On the other hand, many other people with very few material achievements to their credit seem very happy. All happy people, whether materially rich or poor, use the principles of Lasting Purpose in one way or another, either in the form of a religion or as a personal philosophy. Miserable people are not letting love be their master. Most of them, in fact, cannot even understand such a concept and so, in effect, they are irretrievably miserable.

My hope in sharing this wonderful self-healing perspective with you is that you will not only understand it, but consistently apply it as well. The only way to claim this peace and joy for yourself is to actually experience it.

OVERCOMING RESISTANCE

As you set about with new adventures, it is helpful to remember that there is a limited amount of wealth and power in the world, and at any one time, all of it is taken. As a result, when you fill up your cup, you are forced to take power from somebody else's bucket. You should not be surprised, then, if you sometimes get your hand slapped. When you make a million dollars in the stock market and other people lose a million, you cannot expect them to be happy about it.

If you become a world champion in anything, somebody else loses the title. The former world heavyweight boxing champion must hand his coveted title belt over to the new champion who defeats him. Most of the time, those people with power, position and influence will not give them up without a desperate fight. The more power people have, the more obstacles they will put in your path to keep you from getting any of it. Such is the material of many great novels and movies. It is also the material of which real life is made.

When I went up against the captain of the football team and beat him in the practice plays, I walked away with more power and prestige, and he walked away with less. He was very motivated, therefore, to block my pathway to success. Every time another person is converted to chiropractic care, it costs the medical profession thousands or even tens of thousands of dollars in lost revenue. Naturally, organized medicine resists anyone who takes away what they consider to be "their patients" and "their money." When I built a school of chiropractic, thousands of students who would have gone to other colleges or medical schools came to Life College instead. So Life College met resistance from the beginning, and continues to be challenged day after day and year after year.

Lasting Purpose, however, attracts so many friends and supporters to Life College that, in the long run, our detractors are overwhelmed. No matter what worthy goals and objectives you are pursuing, if you go after them with a love-based Lasting Purpose mindset, your friends will always outnumber your enemies. Life College could not exist without its thousands of friends. And we have this wealth of friends because we deserve them: We continue to love, serve and give out of our own abundance.

You should not be discouraged when your goals to acquire wealth and power are met with opposition. The more ambitious your goals, the greater will be the resistance. If a clerk in an office asks the boss for a raise, the clerk is asking that the employer sacrifice some of his or her wealth to make that increase possible. If a junior executive starts making decisions that have always been the prerogative of a senior executive, then he or she is competing with that senior executive for the limited amount of power available in that office. When Wendy's locates a restaurant across the street from McDonald's, which often happens, then a competition for sales, revenue and power ensues. Instances like these are ripe for resistance. Just keep in mind that resistance can nearly always be overcome with focus and persistence. You need to be sure, however, that you are focused on the right thing and persisting in the right direction.

Commitment to Lasting Purpose gives you persistency of purpose to love, serve and give out of your own abundance. This, in turn, gives you more internal love and brings you into better spiritual attunement. You are not centered on yourself and your conscious-minded negativisms. With this focus of Lasting Purpose love, you are more intelligent, more creative and more daring. You are also more likeable. People are attracted to you and enjoy helping you achieve your goals and objectives. When everybody else is butting their heads against a brick wall of formidable obstacles, you will have the inspiration and determination to dare to crawl up and over the wall and see what's on the other side.

BUILDING BELIEF IN YOURSELF

Commitment to Lasting Purpose helps you to believe in yourself, to greatly increase and focus your energies, to greatly increase your productivity and, of course, to accomplish your fondest dreams. Most people waste much of their time on activities that contribute nothing of benefit to others or to their own personal happiness. They don't stay focused on a goal long enough to accomplish it. They hesitate and vacillate so much that they bore a hole in the ground where they are and never get anywhere. They sit at home watching television six to 12 hours a day, escaping to a fantasy land, and wonder why the real world is passing them by. They're just good ol' boys and girls who eke out a living but leave nothing behind except dust, debts and bad memories.

Those people who have tapped into their internal treasure of innate intelligence and who, therefore, know where they want to go and how to get there, will find themselves going from one achievement to another, enjoying their successes, while others spin their wheels on one dead-end side road after another. Once you are able to say to yourself with absolute authority, "I can do this thing and I will do it," that opens up your Innate Subconscious Mind. Then, if you totally submit to it, believing your vision with all your heart, your Innate Subconscious Mind will guide you to achieve your vision.

We are told that when Elvis Presley first auditioned to appear at the Grand Ole Opry, he was flippantly advised by the conservative manager that he should return to truck driving as a career. That did not jibe very well with Elvis' thoughts of "I am a star now." Elvis reportedly smashed his guitar backstage—and went on to become the undisputed "king" of rock-and-roll. If he had not been able to speak, act and sing with authority, he might have let that major rejection discourage him. Instead, he became that much more persistent. In the end, he exceeded even his own ambitions—at least materially.[1]

As you continue to speak to yourself with authority and your confidence builds until you have an absolute belief in yourself and your ability to achieve your goal, you then see yourself in your mind's eye actually achieving your goal. You are able to say with total authority, "I am! I am a football star," or "I am a great salesperson," or "I am a dynamic teacher." When that happens, it's like a jet pilot switching on the afterburners. BOOM! You're there. You have the thoughts and inner direction of a person who has already achieved his or her objective. You have a totally different way of looking at yourself, other people and your current situation. You're no longer a "wanta-be." You are an "I am" person who is achieving and experiencing success right now.

Not only is this new attitude communicated with authority to every cell in your body, but it is communicated to other people as well—from your Innate to theirs. They respect the authority that is created by your firm beliefs, your total commitment and your absolute confidence. At this point, achievement is automatic. You no longer just dream about doing or being. You are.

Tough times can make or break you. Without greatly increased heat and pressure, a diamond would be nothing but a lump of coal. Many people who were pampered as children have turned out to be little more than lumps of common coal; they rarely develop a great enthusiasm for life and almost never make significant achievements. Nearly all "diamond" personalities can look back to great heat and pressure in their formative years.

---

[1] I understand that a writer who interviewed him six weeks before his death pointed out to Elvis that his early ambition had been to be rich, famous and happy. "So, do you feel you have achieved all of those?" the writer asked. Elvis' answer reportedly was, "Actually, I've never been so lonely in my life." His controversial demise bears that out. Yet it is a tribute to his talent that even many years after his death, the popularity of "the King" continues to be a unique phenomenon in the entertainment industry.

When you feel you are doing what you were put here on the earth to do, you develop a sense of purpose and belonging that give vitality and joy to living. Our word "vocation" comes from a Latin root that means "calling." We all enjoy work that we consider our vocation. As we proceed, however, you will learn how to enjoy all work that you choose to do—and even work that is imposed upon you without your asking for it. In a sense, then, you can choose for your calling to be the enjoyment of each moment of each day, regardless of what demands and opportunities the day may bring. Would you not consider that a worthy and rewarding vocation?

3

Building Skills Through Lasting Purpose

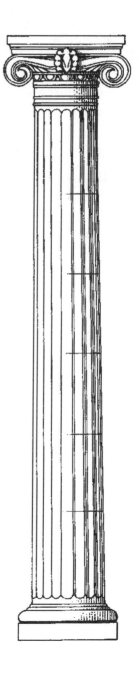

LISTENING TO THE
"WEE SMALL VOICE WITHIN"

In the Lasting Purpose journey, one of the greatest joys comes when you learn to let your conscious mind be still so that you can begin responding positively to that "wee small voice within."[1] This voice inside you is available to guide you, provided you're ready to hear it and pay attention to what it says. It does not shout at you or demand to be heard, so its messages often are not heard at all because of all the chatter of the mind. All too often, even when the messages are heard, they are simply overpowered or ignored and therefore not utilized. With the skill that comes from practice, however, you will find your own inner voice become a working partner and an invaluable aid when you are trying to decide where to go, what to do, and how to accomplish any particular task at hand.

The source of the wee small voice, the repository for all your strong private thoughts, is the Innate Subconscious Mind. In some religions, this kind of communication might be considered the voice of God or promptings by the Holy Spirit. In my experience, I have found nothing to contradict the belief that this inner voice is, indeed, a communication from Universal Intelligence—what some might consider the voice of God speaking to you.

God, in this sense, is like a sea of intelligence surrounding every living creature that provides rules for mankind and the universe to follow. I am not talking about a booming voice that comes from a burning bush, of course. These communications are totally within your own mind, but their ultimate

---

[1] "Wee small voice" is put in quotes because it is not a true human-type voice at all. All we're talking about here are the ideas and directives that come to you as intuitive feelings and subtle revelations.

source is the great Universal Intelligence system that is available to all humans with a mindset for receiving them. What a resource for peace, harmony, love and success for people who learn to be activated by their mindset and allow Universal Intelligence to work through them!

Whether you choose to look at it in the same way or give the phenomenon a more scientific interpretation, the result is the same: You will be much wiser and much more successful in your Lasting Purpose pursuits if you pay attention to the soft proddings of your inner mind in the form of ideas and directions. As you practice this kind of attentiveness, the internally guiding voice will become clearer, and the ideas will become more definite.

Many aspects of Lasting Purpose are neither rational nor reasonable to the conscious mind, which is trained to think that the knowledge that can be poured into it through education is all that counts in life. Lasting Purpose is not the kind of philosophy that you learn in most classrooms. Totally contrary to common logic, Lasting Purpose demands that you love, serve and give out of your own abundance, just for the sake of doing it, with no concern about an immediate return on your investment. You use your vision of what you want to achieve, and persistently "act as if" you are absolutely certain of the achievement in order to establish belief, keep yourself motivated, and keep yourself open to prodding and prompting from your Innate Subconscious Mind, which supplies you with ideas and resources. You never let a temporary defeat discourage you. You work just for the sake of working, continue to speak to yourself with authority, and enjoy the journey whether you reach your destination exactly as planned or not. You appreciate the fact that you are continuously "being paid" by building up your abundance of love and persistency.

There is a story people used to tell when I was a youngster about a little country boy who was seen in a drugstore putting one penny after another into the peanut machine. He would pull the handle, hold out his other hand, and laugh with delight as he raked out the peanuts and put them in his over-alls pockets. When he ran out of pennies, he would go to the cashier and get more change. An elderly gentleman watching him finally asked, "What's that you're so busy doing, son?"

"I'm playing this peanut machine," the little boy responded with a big smile. "And," he continued proudly, "I've hit the jackpot every time I've played it today!"

As an intelligent adult, when you drop coins into a vend-ing machine, you expect the chosen product to come down the chute. You expect that to happen every time, and it almost always does. When you drop a coin into a slot machine in Las Vegas, you hope lots of coins will come out, but you don't expect it to happen every time. Enjoying the benefits of Lasting Purpose is a lot more like playing a slot machine than playing a peanut machine. The big difference is that you don't worry about whether or not you'll hit the jackpot. In child-like innocence, you just play for the fun of playing and enjoy pulling the handle and seeing the wheels go around. If you do hit the jackpot, great! You share the bounty with the people around you, keep enough to continue playing, and go on with the game. That's also the essence of how you live a Lasting Purpose life—with a firm commitment to achieve whatever you set out to do and speaking to yourself with authority to that effect.

You have faith and knowledge, however, that if you keep playing long enough and with enough dedication, always listening to the wee small voice within, you will get many small jackpots along the way. Since you are definitely in the competition, you are aware that you may hit the big jackpot at any time. For some people, that giant jackpot may simply be the joy they feel inside from giving out of their own abundance. When you are truly practicing Lasting Purpose, such a spiritual payoff can be more than adequate. For others, the major purpose may be to become a corporate leader or a world-class athlete. No matter what it is you're reaching for, a Lasting Purpose mindset adds to your skills by developing your connection with the innate intelligence within you that is your "sleeping giant."

When you come to a point in your personal development that material possessions are no longer your raison d'être, or reason for living, but instead are more of a secondary motivation, then your treasury of internal love and internal warmth—made possible by Lasting Purpose giving over the years—becomes increasingly more valuable to you. You're not making just a false gesture with your giving. You are sincere because the feeling of love that is the basis of your giving and serving is being generated and multiplied deep within you, and it continues to build up and to make you increasingly more capable.

If you should reach what you recognize as your final days with very few material possessions but with a great abundance of love, persistency and memories of having lived a helpful, giving, Lasting Purpose life, then you will have few regrets. If, on the other hand, all you have is a huge fortune built upon the misfortunes and misery of others, your exit from this world is not likely to be pleasant. The former can be found in the hearts and minds of the many friends and admirers they leave behind. The latter can be found only in the obituary columns.

Lasting Purpose, under the guidance of the wee small voice

within, provides a true lasting purpose for your life. When you spend your life loving, serving and giving out of your own abundance, by the standards of most religions, you have also served both God and yourself very well indeed. Whether you have lived just a few years or many, you will hear many echoes of "Well done, good and faithful friend!"

PRACTICE MAKES FOR PURPOSE

A child who falls down and skins a knee when learning to ride a bike is temporarily defeated. Yet the child is a failure only if he or she doesn't get up and try again. With Lasting Purpose, you learn to always get up—and to never give up. You can never be beaten, only delayed, because love, like persistency, is its own reward.

It has been said that if you put fleas in a jar, they will immediately start hopping and bumping their heads against the top. After they do this for a while, they stop jumping quite as high to avoid hitting the top. After a few days, you can take the top off and, if the fleas jump at all, they will not jump high enough to escape because they have been conditioned to jump only so high. I have never tested fleas in this manner myself, but it appeals to my logic and serves to illustrate a point: Defeat often is just a state of mind instead of a state of affairs. The fleas could jump out of the jar once the lid is removed, but their horizons are limited in their own minds by their previous failures.

In the same way, for hundreds of years the four-minute mile was an invisible barrier to all runners. It was only when Roger Bannister ran the mile in under four minutes for the first time in recorded history that other athletes began to realize that "there is no lid." Then, within a matter of weeks, hundreds of other runners clocked in at under four minutes. What made the difference? Belief! Once runners started believing they could run the mile in less than four minutes, the belief opened their minds to success. Don't block success with artificial barriers. Believe and you will succeed!

When you are living by the principles of Lasting Purpose, no matter how many obstacles you bump into, you never feel like a failure. You learn from your temporary defeat and move on, always enjoying doing just for the sake of doing, regardless of whether a material reward is immediately forthcoming or not. The material rewards usually do come, of course, and you keep them in your vision, but you regard them more as "bonuses" than as "base salary." Your base salary is the peace and joy that come from entering the silence as you learn to successfully court it, and then enjoying the wisdom and direction of your Innate Subconscious Mind. You are free of all the negative influences of attitudes, thoughts and actions based in hate or fear. Lasting Purpose love sets you free. When you love, serve and give solely for their own sakes, you never feel defeated. With each temporary setback, you get up and try again—and keep on trying again until you succeed.

Lasting Purpose applies to every moment and every behavior of your life. Like learning to drive a car or ride a bicycle, the more you practice Lasting Purpose, the more skillful you become at living it and the more natural it feels. For Lasting Purpose to become truly effective and maximally enriching in your life, it has to become a part of your very nature—a part of your personality that never changes, no matter what circumstances you find yourself in. When Lasting Purpose is truly a mindset for you, it is inviolate; it never changes. It becomes as much a part of your life as breathing.

There is a real challenge to living a loving, serving, giving life even as a cloistered monk. But when you have to deal on a daily basis with ignorance, greed and violence, the test of your philosophical skills is even more difficult. Nevertheless, a Lasting Purpose mindset does not require a pristine external environment for its validation. With a mindset of love, you create your own pleasant internal environment. Lasting Purpose giving creates internal feelings of love, compassion and understanding that encourage camaraderie and create an indomitable attitude of optimism and enthusiasm. Our word "enthusiasm" comes from the Greek word *entheos,* which means "possessed by a god or other superhuman power." Lasting Purpose love is a superhuman power that produces enthusiasm for what you are doing. It also makes you more capable of living an achieving life in the real world.

Lasting Purpose is more than just a positive attitude; it's a complete change in the way you feel and the way you look at life and life's challenges. You are able to think, speak and act with complete authority in every activity of your life. You feel competent because you are.

OPENING THE DOOR TO CREATIVITY

Establishing a Lasting Purpose mindset is as important to creativity as the discovery of the wheel was to transportation. With the commitment to love generated by the establishment of a Lasting Purpose mindset, you flow along with an abundance of energy, persistency and innovative ideas that are light years ahead of anything that can be produced by the trudging, conscious-minded struggle for daily bread and mere survival. Life is more than bread, water and a safe place to sleep.

Whatever you choose to do, do it just for the joy of doing it. Learn to enjoy the process, focusing on the joy of loving

and giving, with no great conscious concern about the end
product as such, knowing that you can and will receive material rewards at the right time. With Lasting Purpose, you are
able to create a strong, significant spiritual presence about you
that attracts people. You emit what people perceive as leadership, and that fulfills a need for them. You've got a made-up
mind. You've found your internal answer, and it is evident in
your bearing. Furthermore, you're in contact with an internal
source of wisdom that, although available to all, is accessed by
only the few who have learned to knock at this internal door
and give up their dependence on conscious, external, educated thinking. Most people are trained to try to "out-think"
others, using their limited conscious minds. They do not
know to knock at the innate door that will give them the best
answers.

Doing just for the sake of doing is a concept that is often
rejected and ridiculed when it's first encountered. It runs contrary to the attitude of "What's in it for me?" When you begin
putting the Lasting Purpose principles to work in your daily
life, however, you soon appreciate the wisdom of this system,
as it brings peace, joy and satisfaction—as well as achievement
and accomplishment—to your life.

Most people will fight you to keep you from forcefully taking their money or power away from them, but when they see
that your sincere goal is to serve them and others, they are
eager to give you whatever you need. By speaking to yourself
with authority and "acting as if," you also are able to act with
authority and reach out and grab the vision that you have generated in your mind's eye, all the while enjoying each moment
that leads to momentary bursts of victory.

Once you have matured in your Lasting Purpose way of
life, and as you continue to speak to yourself with authority,

the stream of directives from your Innate Subconscious Mind can be utilized to accomplish your various practical, everyday goals and objectives. This internal wisdom can help you in getting a better job, expanding your business, or winning the love and companionship of a worthy and compatible person. You continue to practice the core of Lasting Purpose—loving, serving and giving—but with another part of your mind, you are able to be alert to opportunities and to walk through those doors when they are opened.

THE POWER OF SHARING

We have all heard that "it is better to give than to receive." Yet most people either do not understand this concept or cannot accept it, as it appears to be in direct conflict with the usual principles for success. A lot of "experts" are teaching that you should look out for yourself first and seek to win out over others through intimidation at any cost. This is the kind of attitude that produces criminal behavior, economic chaos, divorces, runaway children and wars.

The principles of Lasting Purpose reveal to you the more reliable secret of the power of sharing. It means you give from your abundance of love and other resources, only to find those resources increased instead of depleted as the law of just returns begins to operate in your life. It is through the power of sharing with others that I have been able to achieve repeated successes in the face of what often seemed to be overwhelming odds.

You don't have to give away all your money just because you're giving from your abundance. Often the things most valuable to others cost you nothing—a friendly smile, a warm handshake, some words of praise and encouragement. When you constantly, consistently and sincerely give of yourself in such a way, you become known as a dynamic, positive person who is pleasant to be around. With that kind of personality and reputation, plus the ever-increasing love and persistency that are building up inside you, you have the foundation for gaining the cooperation you need for any kind of project that you, with your Lasting Purpose mindset, are enthusiastic about.

4

Formulas for Success

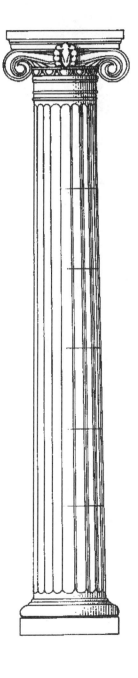

COURTING THE SILENCE

In order for the Lasting Purpose mindset to be effective for you, you must apply it to every facet of your daily life. If you practice Lasting Purpose with routine daily events, then when the big challenges come along—as they do for all of us—you will be fortified by an inner abundance of love and persistency needed to help you intelligently persevere and be successful.

The process for learning to live a Lasting Purpose life is so simple that it seems complex. It's hard for somebody who has not experienced it to really believe it is so elementary. A strategy you can use to get started is to begin to be aware of your thought flashes.

Like a bubble slowly rising from the bottom of a pond, a thought flash is a communication that filters up from deep within the Innate Subconscious Mind to your conscious mind. The thought flash is sometimes poetically referred to as "an inspiration from the gods." It is creative intelligence in capsule form. When a solution to a problem you've been working on seems to come to you "out of the blue," you need to recognize and appreciate that as a thought flash. Then begin to keep your mind innately attuned to receiving more thought flashes. The more you tune into and value your thought flashes, the more often they will come and the higher will be their quality.

After you become intimately acquainted with thought flashes and feel comfortable with relying upon this Innate Subconscious intelligence, you should find yourself desiring to take a further step of being guided on a more consistent basis by your Innate Subconscious. You do this by courting the silence, a technique for cultivating thought flashes. When you court the silence, you allow your conscious mind to be distracted. You encourage it to be turned off to a lot of negative bombardment—anxiety, fear, frustration, hate, envy, greed, competitiveness, etc. Then, every once in a while, there comes a "gap" or hiatus in your consciousness. When that happens, you don't have anything at all going on in your conscious mind. This is the silence I'm talking about.

Inner silence is always available to you, but it requires that you welcome it and be prepared to connect with it. You plug into it. When a gap comes, you get into the gap. You don't create the gap; it's just there. The bombardment may continue through you, but it doesn't bother you because you're attuned to the silence, and the more you stay in the silence, the stronger it becomes. When properly used, this elevated state of consciousness that you can achieve makes it possible for you to improve the quality of your life in general. It removes stress and eliminates your addiction to anxiety, hate, resentment, greed, jealousy, avarice, fear and other negative subconscious bombardments that usually are the product of conscious-minded thinking.

By courting the silence, which is simply waiting for that vacuum or period of nothingness in your conscious thinking, you get enough space between thoughts so you create longer periods of bliss to implant a new way of life. With training and persistency, always speaking to yourself with authority to establish belief, your mind can come to be dominated and ruled on a day-to-day basis by this new habit.

Herman Melville once said, "Silence is the only voice of our God." He obviously understood the rewards of courting the silence. There is no way to fully express the power of it. Like seeing a sunset or hearing the song of a bird, it's something you, yourself, have to do at least once to understand and appreciate and claim as your own.

A lot of people feel threatened by the basically "blank" state of mind they experience when they are successful in courting the silence. They get scared when they find themselves in a situation where they don't have some kind of noise going on, so they look for somebody to talk to or they turn on a radio or TV. If nothing else is available, they may even start talking to themselves or whistling. They feel lonesome for all that "mind noise" or chatter that they're used to having, even though most of it serves them no useful purpose.

However, to be able to lock onto the pursuit of new goals and objectives and tap into the full use of your Innate Subconscious Mind, you have to learn to be patient, to be persistent, and to seek that mystical inner silence. Just wait for that blank space in your thinking, and when you find it, do whatever is needed to cling to it and stay silent, avoiding the noise. That is how you come to enjoy the peacefulness and euphoria produced by those gaps in your conscious thinking.

To be successful in courting the silence, you must be patient and understand the value of just persistently waiting. If you were a child watching an egg so you could see the baby chick hatch, you would have to apply this same kind of patience. As you watched and listened, eventually you would hear a soft tapping. The sound would continue to grow louder and then, suddenly, a little beak would pierce the eggshell. If you were impatient to see the chick, you might be tempted to help the little fellow by peeling the egg yourself. If you did, you could very well cause irreparable damage to the chick and its natural development. Nature intended for the chick to do its own hatching out, and build up its strength and coordination in the process. So it is with the silence. When you sense it's coming, don't pick at it! Just wait and let nature take its course.

In time, as you continue to talk positively and firmly to

yourself with complete authority and gain skill in entering and holding onto the silence, it soon becomes possible for you to experience a continuous stream of internal directions coming from your Innate Subconscious Mind. This is what I call "being in the flow." In its highest level of perfection, you are able to reach the "divine latitude," which is very fragile and will not tolerate even the slightest distraction, whether positive or negative.

At whatever level you are able to achieve it, this stream of Innate guidance helps you continue to be a Lasting Purpose person while also pursuing your most desired material goals and objectives in life. Your innate subconscious thoughts then root out and overwhelm the trivia being processed by the conscious mind, as the "warrior within" manages your life in a more purposeful, focused, peaceful and rewarding manner. You are able to express spiritual love more freely and to exercise persistency from your own abundance in a natural, spontaneous way. You can also then begin to recognize, appreciate and confidently depend upon thought flashes as a source of creativity and as a reliable solution to problems. I realize now that, whether I was a youngster learning to throw a knife or a 139-pound Georgia Tech end meeting blockers head-on and tackling opponents as much as half again my size, I was always propelled to success by powerful words and images that pulsed through my body and mind like a heartbeat.

To begin with, you may not be able to maintain the silence for more than a few seconds. Don't be discouraged! Over time, with love and persistency, your skills will improve. After decades of practice, I find it very satisfying now to be able to go along for hours and even days with nothing occupying my awareness but the deep, spiritual fulfillment that is a part of being in the silence. Even though I am carrying on my regular personal and business activities, I am not bothered by any negative emotions.

At a state of oneness with my higher self (my Innate), and in constant spiritual communication with the sea of intelligence that many call God, I am, in effect, "praying without ceasing." Yet this process is not something I do, but rather, something I undo. I undo the world and all its negative influences and just allow love to love through me. Without deliberately doing anything, I simply let the silence and the state of bliss it produces enter and remain undisturbed.

Since your desired mindset should be one of selfless, unconditional love and eternal, unilateral persistency, any positive, authoritative statement to support and confirm that mindset will help you develop those practices. By engaging in loving, supportive, nurturing actions; sharing positive, encouraging words with others at every opportunity; and courting the silence, a true Lasting Purpose mindset can become engraved upon your subconscious mind. Eventually, it can even become a comfortable habit. That habit, along with irresistible desire and the practice of speaking to yourself with authority, is one of the primary keys to success. Your new way of life then permits sincere acts of loving, serving and giving; eliminates the self-defeating fraud of pretending and play-acting; and provides you with the innate resources to fearlessly accomplish your dreams and desires.

REALIZING A VISION

Very early in my life, when I first heard about the so-called power of positive affirmations, I rejected the idea because nobody told me exactly how to utilize the system or why it should work. As I know now, just repeating phrases over and over, as though you were casting some magic spell, is of very little value. Mentally repeating instructions to yourself is strictly a left-brain activity. If, however, you use affirmations to speak to yourself with such irresistible authority that another part of your mind begins to believe your affirmations and is able to visualize your goal being achieved, then you also are drawing upon your right-brain resources. This produces a very powerful whole-brain effort.

So the most effective success formula is this: When you have generated an intense desire to accomplish some objective, then repeat to yourself with absolute authority, "I can do this, I will do this, I must do this," until you sincerely believe it and are able to visualize yourself actually achieving what you desire. When you say "I can," that is just a shorthand way of saying, "I have the intelligence, the talent and the fortitude to do this. If anybody can do it, I can!" "I will" simply summarizes your firm resolution and demonstrates your made-up mind. You are saying, "I will pay the price, whatever it takes. Nothing will deter me. No sacrifice is too great." Then, only if you feel your resolve slipping, you may have to call upon the affirmation of "I must!" As you catch a glimpse of possible defeat, you remind yourself of the cost of failure and use that incentive to spur yourself on to victory.

Eventually, you will find yourself saying with absolute confidence, "I am!" You don't have to speak out loud, of course, but to be effective, the words at least must be repeated obsessively in your head and with uncompromising authority. And when your image of yourself succeeding begins to appear, you want to make it as clear and convincing as possible. At that point, the resources of your Innate Subconscious Mind are accessed and your Innate begins to work for you, sending you continuous messages to help you collect the needed resources and to direct you in accomplishing your objectives. The cry of "I must" is then almost never needed again because your belief in yourself is so firm, and your image of victory so clear, that a thought of failure is unlikely to be able to penetrate your consciousness. Like a house coming together one board at a time, your goal begins to take shape. As you listen to the wee small voice in your head, you build your vision until what you see in the physical world is what you have long seen in your own mind's magic eye. That is what is called "realizing a vision." It feels good.

BEWARE THE ROAR OF THE ENGINE

I have often been asked if this power to transcend the conventional parameters of time, space and energy to achieve results that, to most others, seem all but impossible, can ever be lost. My answer is an emphatic yes! Many powerful and talented people, from the biblical Samson to modern-day politicians and business leaders, have forsaken their power by giving in to a lust that kills their connection with an all-consuming and energizing love.

In my earlier days, when I was looking for answers wherever I could find them, I was fascinated by a faith healer who had established quite a reputation for his talent at "laying on of hands." I wanted to see what he was doing and how he did it. As I continued to attend his services for several days, sitting up front and putting a few dollars in the hat each time it was passed around, he and I came to be acquainted, and I had the privilege of asking him some personal questions. One thing I inquired about was whether he had ever lost the power.

This evangelistic healer said he had been in prayer and under God's will for a long time and that his ministry was doing great. He said God would heal people through him instantaneously, with just the simple laying on of his hands. Then he said, "One day the devil tempted me." He had looked out the window of his office and had seen this beautiful red convertible parked on the street. He was so entranced by it that he went downstairs and persuaded the owner to let him sit in it. Sitting in the soft, luxurious front seat and smelling all the rich newness of this very expensive car, he continued to be swept up by the magnetic attraction of this perfect symbol of materialistic worldliness. Unable to resist further, he asked the owner if he could start it up. The owner handed him the key. He put it in the switch and turned it. "The moment I felt the roar of the engine in my body," he said, "I lost it. The power of the Lord left me. I couldn't have healed a pair of chapped lips with a gallon of Vaseline. It took me six months of praying, fasting and sincere repentance before I got the power back."

The message here is that once you receive "the pearl of great price," you must keep it in a safe place—in a heart and mind totally immersed in and protected from any distraction. Whether a distraction is based in love, hate or fear, it's all the same. The preacher loved the new car, but that material love was in conflict with his "spiritual contract" with God. Anything that takes your mind off your main business at hand of loving, serving and giving out of your own abundance can wreck your Lasting Purpose mindset. As discussed earlier, extraneous material pursuits must be attended to very carefully with "the other hand" and "another part of your mind" if you want to stay in the flow and maintain continuous communication with your inner voice.

As you have seen, this is a story about love. It's not about two people being "in love," but it's about that magical ingredient that so many people readily admit is missing from their lives. The story of Lasting Purpose is about releasing the love that has always been within you and will always be within you. It is a story about getting that love activated and so thoroughly woven into your everyday life that love is your master and rules your life. Letting this internally-generated love rule your life then enables you to speak and act with overwhelming authority. Ultimately, this elevated degree of consciousness dominated by love helps produce for you the highest possible level of achievement and respect that you desire.

5

Profiting from Lessons Learned

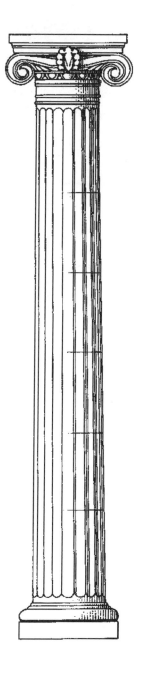

IMMERSING YOUR CONSCIOUS MIND IN LOVE

As you read earlier, my Lasting Purpose life actually began when I was a little boy learning how to throw a knife. You also shared my later adventure in which I finally was able to speak to myself with authority, to establish belief in myself and unleash this great abundance of love within me. As you will remember, this phenomenon occurred when, with no conscious intention by me, an accidental distraction allowed me to tap into that natural resource and, for the first time, experience an all-consuming, compelling love for a product I was trying to sell.

Since that fortuitous event, almost every day of my life has continued to be one of joyful discovery and accomplishment, as I have repeated this experience of being "loved through" and being "worked through" by the higher, more subtle powers within me. What this meant was giving up my educated, conscious control of my thoughts and actions and allowing my wiser, more sublime Innate Subconscious Mind to direct my life, bringing forth and radiating outward to others the Love that was within me.

Some may consider this as "knowing God's presence" in their life. Whatever you choose to call it, once you master this skill of accessing the love within you, you'll have the comfort of knowing that you are sharing a great part of the secrets known and shrouded by monks and saints of various religions throughout the world. These various mystics reach out to powers beyond their own limited conscious mind by reaching deeply into the powers within their own Innate Subconscious Mind. So can you.

The primary objective of Lasting Purpose is to help you understand, adopt and perfect the principles of letting this enchanting, magnetic love flow from deep within your inner being so you then automatically and naturally allow love to love through you and express itself in your everyday activities. At the same time, you also are always being persistent, if only to build up your natural resource of persistency.

As you have seen, the development of a focused, persistent, loving consciousness generated by desire and the ability to speak with authority is an extremely potent force. It almost always guarantees success. This force can be seen more clearly in lower animals. Ants, for example, are very simplistic in their thought processes. They do not wake up in the morning, write out a "to do" list, and then visualize all the reasons the goals cannot be achieved. Ants by nature are very limited in their choices. They just get up and get on with the job that their innate intelligence tells them to do. They apparently do not have any conscious minds to tell them they can't do something. If they meet an obstacle along the way to harvesting a caterpillar or a piece of candy, they go around the obstacle, through it, over it or under it. Short of death, they cannot be stopped. When you choose to put yourself under the control of your Innate Subconscious Mind, you can overcome one of your major human weaknesses and allow yourself to possess this same power of achievement.

Your conscious-minded self is not able to access this Lasting Purpose love on its own. Your educated-mind consciousness, in fact, is like a dry sponge, totally devoid of spiritual love. However, when you develop the ability to allow your conscious mind to be distracted, so that the love within your Innate Subconscious Mind can manifest itself, then you can allow your total being to be saturated in love. You become like a sponge immersed in the ocean. You become full of love. In the same way that the sponge is in the ocean and the ocean is in the sponge, so are you in a vast ocean of spiritual love that fills the universe and the minds of all other living entities. That same spiritual love is also eternally in you. If you take the saturated sponge and touch your hand with it, your hand soaks up some of the ocean's wetness, as the water from the ocean comes through the sponge to wet your skin. In the same way, when you are saturated with love, a little of it rubs off on everything you touch. The people around you feel the love as it passes through you to them. That is what I mean by "being loved through." It is not your love any more than the ocean is the sponge's ocean. You are a vehicle—a conduit—for distributing this vast abundance of love that is in you and in which you have learned to immerse yourself with a Lasting Purpose mindset. This elevated level of love-based consciousness gives you a presence that sometimes is thought of as "charisma." This magnetic presence, in turn, opens hearts and doors—a phenomenon that helps turn your dreams into reality.

APPLYING THE MAGIC POTION

Once I came to understand the power of love and how to utilize it deliberately, anytime thereafter that I made sales calls, it was as though I mesmerized my clients. It took very few words to secure an appointment and, with that done, a sale was then almost a certainty. I was the Bruce Valentine of cookware! With each new prospect, I would begin asking leading questions that ultimately would culminate in a commitment to purchase. I noticed that when I was in this love-directed state of consciousness, almost everything I said was aimed at motivating the prospect to take progressive steps toward signing an order. I was consistently strong and intense, almost to the point of being overwhelming. On each sales call, when I picked up that little saucepan and caressed it with loving regard, I expected and usually heard accolades for the product from my client's own mouth. Within a few minutes, as though a magic potion had been cast into the air we breathed, both the client and I would be caught up in a state of ecstasy as the order form was being happily signed. Once a sale was made under these circumstances, it was almost never canceled. Needless to say, I raked in the money—enough to finance the rest of our education at Palmer once I turned my attention back to my studies. My grades went back up and Dr. Nell and I both graduated on schedule.

It was this intimate innate knowledge, gained from that first accidental introduction to the power of love and released by the distraction of my mind, that has propelled me from one success to another. From that time on, by applying methodical persistency, coupled with intense desire and speaking to myself with complete authority to generate belief, whatever I wanted was mine. I had learned that when you have love, you can accomplish anything that you really believe you can accomplish. And to believe, all you have to do is learn to speak to yourself with unyielding authority. With this focus, once you begin to believe, in your mind's eye you can see yourself as having already completed your project. So you are able to continue to act and speak with complete authority, which also draws people and resources to you like a magnet. It is a wondrously mysterious metaphysical process that can only be fully understood by applying it and learning it through constant submission to its demands.

As you will agree once you experience it, the power that was directing me as I was swept away by love for that little saucepan appears to be the same power possessed by great achievers in many disciplines. Elvis Presley had it. John F.

Kennedy had it. So did Franklin Delano Roosevelt. Frank Sinatra still has it, as does Billy Graham. It's more than charisma. When you learn to talk to yourself with authority until you are able to believe, and then think and act with total submission to the euphoric state of mind that total dedication to a purpose and being loved through gives you, there is an aura about you that makes people pay attention to you. They are pulled to you and feel compelled to help you—even though they may have no idea why.

Love in the possession of one who walks and talks with authority is, indeed, "a many splendored thing." It must be treated tenderly, of course, because the attitude of "being loved through" is very demanding and is resentful of conflicting interests. Nevertheless, if you cherish and nurture it, you will never walk alone.

ACHIEVING YOUR OWN HEAVEN ON EARTH

Obviously, Lasting Purpose is not ruled by gifts of money or other material things. But neither is it made up only of compassionate thoughts and deeds. It's simply achieving a state of consciousness so that, at an off-moment of distraction, overwhelming love can release itself from within you. It then begins to fill your consciousness and totally saturate your whole physical, mental and spiritual being. Once saturated with love, if you allow this transcendent state of mind to very carefully and delicately handle and guide you, this innate control can last for days, months or even years without significant interruption. It can dominate your life and have a positive influence on all whose paths intersect yours.

This "heaven on earth" can be achieved in many different ways, but never without a foundation of internally-generated love. It is considered by many as "the pearl of great price." It is a gift they would not trade for all the material riches in the world. The everyday internal rewards of practicing these principles are self-evident. However, as you continue to allow love, persistency, focus and speaking with authority to be an integral and overwhelming part of your everyday life, the various opportunities to accomplish the material objectives that may be among your ambitions in life begin to appear.

There are many ways to achieve material riches, but most of them fail to produce happiness and peace of mind. With Lasting Purpose, you are able to achieve the best of both the physical and the spiritual worlds. You can have wealth, power and renown and still sleep like a contented baby every night, never troubled by such peace-robbers as fear of retribution, jealousy, greed, envy or desire for revenge.

Many people find it hard to believe that freely and sincerely giving out of your own abundance of love and other resources actually triggers a natural law that returns to you more than you give. The mysteries of this phenomenon have been known by wise ones since the beginning of civilization. We will explore it in more detail in the next chapter.

6

Taking In, Casting Out

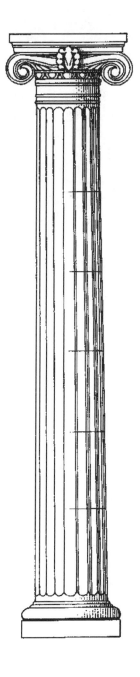

BREAKING THE PROTECTIVE BUBBLE

Fortunately, most people in the world are basically good. If that were not the case, civilized, democratic societies could not exist. Yet not all good people are happy with their lot in life. There are, in fact, some fine human beings who are highly moral, ethical and professional, and who go about living a "good life," being productive and harming no one . . . and yet they still feel fearful, lonely, rejected and unappreciated.

And what about the people who are not all that good but not all that "bad," either? Shouldn't they be happy most of the time? Why do so many people endure a miserable existence filled with hate, greed, envy, jealousy, fear, rejection and frustration? Why do most of them just accept such conditions as their appointed lot in life?

Just "being good," whether some of the time or all of the time, is not the same as living a loving, serving and giving Lasting Purpose life. Some people think that all they have to do is tithe at their church or give huge sums of money to charities, and that will buy them happiness in this life as well as in a spiritual life after death. This is just not true. To be truly happy, you must make a positive, proactive effort to give of yourself every moment of every day. Building up material treasures alone will not bring happiness because happiness comes not from getting, but from giving.

Many individuals appear to be kind, good-hearted, sensitive, loving and always willing to do what's required of them; but when the bell rings and they go off the clock, their giving stops immediately. As time goes on, they find that such giving-to-get behavior does not produce friends, so they're lonely. They think they've given their all and deserve more, so they cannot understand why their efforts are not being "justly" rewarded. Consequently, they turn their backs on the people they think are hurting them and become ever more reclusive. Some eventually become totally paranoid and hide themselves away from the world.

How could such an awful thing happen to basically "good" people? The answer lies in the fact that when you give of yourself only for the rewards it might bring, you will rarely be pleased with what you get. In order for your giving to bring happiness, you must give of yourself unconditionally, doing just for the sake of doing, with no expectation of any additional, external reward. The reward is in your heart and mind. Most people go around every day with a barrier around them that's like a large, plastic bubble. The bubble protects them from the world. It keeps others from knowing what they're really thinking and feeling, and it keeps others from getting emotionally or physically too close. When they wish to make an exchange with the outside world, they open up a little tiny door in their barrier bubble, push out their offering and then, as though operating a vending machine, wait for their reward.

The natural law of return doesn't work that way. You might put out a lot of effort one day and get little or nothing back. But you can't be discouraged by that. You are not seeking an immediate reaction; you are giving out of the biggest door possible just for the sake of giving. And regardless of what you get back any particular day, you continue to do everything possible to widen the door so that you can give even more the next day. When you give unselfishly of yourself, there is always a risk, of course, that your gift will be either refused or abused. Still, the price for giving stingily or not giving at all is more than anyone would willingly and knowingly pay.

You receive through the same door through which you give. Little-door givers should not be surprised when the world is stingy toward them. As a big-door giver, you should also not be surprised to find the world being extraordinarily generous to you.

If you really want to be successful, you need to blast such a big door in the barrier bubble that restricts your giving that, in effect, you have no barrier at all. I couldn't get through the day if I had to give and take measured amounts of love through a door of any size. I like to be able to just reach out and love, serve and give out of my own abundance in any and all directions—sometimes in all directions at once. When I'm giving of myself in a lecture format, for example, whether motivational or otherwise, I'm giving to the people in front of me, in back of me, and even to the people who are not there. I place no limits on the distribution of my love. I let love itself love through me and love everybody and everything.

Giving through a big door is always better than giving through a little door, but as you continue making your door bigger and bigger, eventually you will find you can just throw the whole protective bubble off and forget about it. You become so innately attuned that you have no fear of what may occur, so you need no protection. With your Lasting Purpose mindset, you just continue to operate with a happy, peaceful state of mind that attracts other people to you and helps you to build up supportive relationships. Then when the mother lode of good returns does come your way, you'll have the means to receive them. Your rewards will not have to come through a little door or even a big door. You will not have any barriers to interfere with the receipt of your rewards.

That is the ultimate state of mind when you become skilled in operating with a Lasting Purpose mindset. It takes time, of course, to achieve that sublime level, but with patience and belief generated by speaking to yourself with authority, your time will come. And it will be worth the waiting.

GIVING AND GETTING THROUGH A BIG DOOR

As you continue to work toward the degree of actualization you desire, no doubt there will be setbacks from time to time. Don't let little temporary failures and disappointments destroy your state of mind. Remember, you always have a choice. You choose to fail or succeed. "Good luck" is simply what happens to people who choose to succeed and believe without a doubt that they will.

Always keep in mind that you are not your emotions, your desires or your triumphs. And neither are you your failures. You're bigger than any of these things. All those petty annoyances are like fleas on a dog. The fleas are not the dog—and if the dog scratches hard enough or goes and sits in the creek long enough, it can get rid of the fleas. With a little effort in the form of speaking positively to yourself with great authority until belief is established, you can also overcome those factors that cause a negative, unproductive state of mind.

If you choose to live a loving, serving, giving life for a while and get your feelings hurt, you may be tempted to start closing up your giving door. If you yield to that negative emotion, you are still making a choice: You are choosing to shut out the opportunity for future returns. Fear and hate always serve to close up the giving-getting door and make it small. Your big door is kept wide open by allowing love to be your master.

With the kind of giving I'm talking about, you are just letting the gift of love flow through you. That's the gift you're giving—the gift of love. If you've got the gift of love in you, it comes out all by itself. You can't hold it in. It just flows out—not from you, but through you.

A fearful or hating person's reward, of course, has to come back through that same tiny little door through which he or she gives; so naturally, the return on that person's tiny invest-ment will always be small, too. And that's why so many good people are not happy. Out of hate and fear and ignorance, they choose to give stingily of themselves through such a small door that the love they get back is totally inadequate to meet their own needs.

A good metaphor for this process can be found at the gas stations in high-crime areas of our larger cities. Typically, because of the fear of being robbed, a clerk is enclosed in a bulletproof glass cage. The clerk's only connection with the outside world is a little door at the bottom of the glass where a customer can shove in money and get change back. If you wanted to purchase a carton of soft drinks from this kind of place, you'd be out of luck. A carton of drinks won't fit through the little door. That's reasonable, logical and obvious, so nobody ever tries to get a carton of drinks through the little door. And yet, millions of people every day poke a little offering of love through the tiny door in their own personal barrier bubble and expect to get a huge sackful of love in return. They seem never to figure out that they receive through the same door through which they give; so it's impos-sible to be a "little-door giver" and a "big-door getter."

There is no prison so dark or lonely as the one you make for yourself when you choose to live with hate and fear as your masters.

When you choose to have a little door for loving, serving and giving, you are volunteering to be in a lonely dungeon. Just picture in your mind's eye one of those dark, damp prison cells that were common hundreds of years ago. Some had no windows at all, and only a tiny little door through which food and water was shoved. The prisoner could not have compan-ionship with other people, could not reach out and give comfort to or receive it from another human being. The prisoner could not give or receive love. When you choose a little-door life, you are choosing to put yourself in this same kind of inaccessible prison cell.

On the other hand, if you choose to be like a castle with a huge double door that will allow a whole army to march through, you can have wonderful, loving exchanges with the world that will bring you continuous joy and good fortune.

From time to time, you have no doubt heard of people who were trapped in a burning building by burglar bars and, as a result, were killed by the fire. The steel bars they chose to put on their doors and windows were intended to protect them from harm. Ironically, however, the bars made a reality out of the person's worst fear. Even though would-be rescuers tried to help, they could not get past the bars in time. The same thing happens when, out of hate or fear, you choose to cut yourself off from the world with a little-door attitude. Even though mentally and spiritually you are dying the worst kind of death, people who have the ability and desire to help you can't get through to you. Through your own choice, you've shut yourself up in a prison cell that can only be unlocked from the inside.

When you choose to live the Lasting Purpose life, you choose to give and get through the biggest door possible. There is no limit to your giving or to your achievements. Why would anybody want to live any other way?

CASTING OUT HATE AND FEAR

Neither hate nor fear can long abide the light of love. The law of just returns is as real as the law of gravity. If, like old Ebenezer Scrooge in the classic Christmas story, you have a miserly attitude in your dealings with people—rarely giving deserved praise, never paying fair wages and never forgiving even the least fault or mistake—then you are giving through a little door. What you get from life will come back through that same little door. Typically under those circumstances, you will find life to be unrewarding, fearful and, oftentimes, very lonely. You may even begin to think people are crossing the street to keep from having to meet you. What few friends you have might even drift away from you and be attracted to other, more giving people.

On the other hand, if, like the repentant Scrooge, you are always looking for opportunities to love, serve and give—going that extra mile, smiling, praising, building up and cheering up, not even thinking about what's in it for you—then you're giving through a big castle-like door, and you will receive a great abundance back through that same door. People will just naturally love you and want to be in your presence and honor you. They'll fall all over one another trying to do things for you. You'll build up relationships and multiply and expand your base of contacts to achieve your Lasting Purpose goals. The people who are attracted to you will help raise you to a position of great authority and responsibility because you have demonstrated the main characteristics of leadership. And you'll be happy—I guarantee it. There will be no fear in your heart because "Perfect love casteth out fear." It also casts out hate.

When love is allowed to love through you, it leaves a trail of joy. I'm not saying, of course, that you have to love everybody you meet. I'm not even saying you have to love your particular job, the career field you're in, the company you work for, the school you attend, or anything else. With your Lasting Purpose mindset, what you're doing is performing loving behaviors and activities required by Lasting Purpose. You love giving; being cooperative, kind and helpful; persevering and contributing; being useful; making other people feel good and helping them to be better human beings; being in control of yourself; having a positive attitude; and so forth. As you go through your day—loving, serving and giving out of your own abundance, just enjoying the doing of these things—you build up love and persistency, and that's where your joy comes from. As you become ever more skilled and proficient at everything you do (as you inevitably will), your joy likewise increases.

A lot of times, though, the people you're around or the environment you're in may be repulsive to you. Still, you keep on generating your love signals and beaming them out in the same way that the sun and rain benefit evil people as well as good people. You don't discriminate. You don't have to like people or their behaviors to keep giving of your love in their presence. A radio signal goes out to limousines and clunkers alike, and to both castles and hovels. That's the way you have to beam out your love energy—unconditionally and without discrimination. You cannot love and hate selectively. To truly love, you must love without condition.

There are a few people in the world who seem to be able to have warm, affectionate feelings for every person they meet, regardless of who that person is or what behavior he or she is engaged in. They can smile lovingly at a mugger pointing a gun in their face. These rare, gifted people are qualified to be called "saints." Of course, you don't have to be able to achieve this high degree of spiritual perfection to be happy and successful. As long as you can learn to continue loving, serving and giving, regardless of what situation you're in or what other people around you are doing, you're doing all that's necessary to achieve Lasting Purpose happiness and success.

A key ingredient of the Lasting Purpose mindset is sincerity. The only person you deceive with insincere giving is yourself. You might not like a person you're opening a door for, but you sincerely enjoy the behavior of opening that door. When that person fails to thank you for your courtesy, you are not fazed; you continue to enjoy what you're doing. And you achieve this attitude by sincerely loving, serving and giving out of your own abundance. There's no hypocrisy in that. There is, in fact, great wisdom in that system . . . and great power as well.

These principles apply in all aspects of life. You can't be a Lasting Purpose lover and giver in one part of your daily routine and then be just the opposite in another. Some people try it and fail miserably. They spend their day spitting out honey-coated words, helping people on with their coats, laughing at every joke—all with the me-first purpose of making a sale or getting some other monetary reward. Then they come home and treat their spouses and children in an unloving manner. They may even physically abuse their families. On a short-term basis, such people might succeed in a business or profession. They might even make a lot of money and be considered wealthy and successful by others like them. But are they happy? Not likely. The natural laws governing loving, serving and giving are like the IRS: sooner or later, they'll catch up with you. Your best bet is to have the love you "owe" taken out of your "check" every day, rather than letting the debt build up to a point where you can't afford to pay it.

You might be able to fool most people for a short time, but you can't fool the laws of nature even for a moment. Even if you have the money and power of the late Howard Hughes, unless you have learned to give through a big door, your power is really of no value because you have not learned how to be happy. In spite of all his wealth and his ability to buy and sell other people, Hughes reportedly lived a miserable life and died a pathetic death. Angry power without happiness is the stuff of which wars are made. Happy power feeds on itself and produces a storm of happiness that rains joy on all in its path. If you've always been a sincere giver of yourself and you truly understand what that means, you are very fortunate. I would encourage you to continue to give and receive through that big castle door and enjoy the abundant life that you no doubt have and deserve. If you've begun to realize that there's more Ebenezer Scrooge in you than you'd like there to be, however, don't give up. There's still hope. Remember, the problem is inside you. And that means the solution is inside you, too.

Actually, if you've always lived a "little-door life," the more miserable you are now, the better. Since you've made a prisoner of yourself, you probably feel like a prisoner. Fortunately, however, misery generates desire, which is one of the main factors required for a new focused, made-up mind. As you would use a lemon to make lemonade, use your misery to generate the motivation you need to get the job done. Tell yourself with absolute authority, "I can do better. I can have a Lasting Purpose mindset and love, serve and give out of my own abundance on a consistent basis. I can, I will, I must!" Eventually, as the belief is accepted by another part of your mind, the conviction of "I am" will bubble up into your conscious mind, and you will be able to see the vision of your success in your mind's eye. You will know it is so . . . and it will be so.

CHOOSING TO HAVE OR HAVE NOT

Deep self-analysis is not something you want to do very often in your life. In many cases, what you find is disappointing and of little value. This one time, however, to build up your desire for a different lifestyle, consider taking a hard, honest, realistic look at where you are in your relationships with others around you. The errors most difficult to see, of course, are the ones you make yourself. However, if your mate and children seem not to love you or have long since abandoned you, if your other relatives don't even notify you of funerals, if you have no friends and your boss only tolerates you because you work cheap, and if your dog goes next door when you get home, it would be hard for you to deny that you have a problem! The first step in solving that problem is to admit that you've been giving through a little door. The second step is to start giving through a big door. It's that simple.

Happiness is a choice. If you are not now happy but want to be, then make a conscious decision to change. If you want to change your emotions, you change your state of mind— meaning you rise above your emotions. You can choose to have a happy, successful, peaceful state of mind regardless of what is going on around you.

Peace and happiness do not come from a place you visit. They come from inside your own mind. Happiness and peace represent a state of mind that you choose to have or choose not to have. Once you realize this, it will give you a great sense of power because you will actually possess the ability to control your own life.

One way to start putting your new state of mind to work is to just go ahead and choose to conduct your life as though you have permanently "turned over a new leaf." Be a new person!

Tell yourself with absolute authority, "I can, I will, I must!" Keep telling yourself that until you believe it and find yourself saying, "I am a new person right now, today!"

If you've been watching the clock at work and rushing out the door at 4:55, try ignoring the clock. Work for another half hour or so. Put your desk in shape and make out your agenda for the next day. Smile at the boss when you're leaving and ask if he or she needs anything else before you go. Before you leave, call ahead and tell your spouse to forget about making dinner—you're taking the family out to eat. Then take your spouse and kids to a place they want to go and let them eat what they want to eat. Go the extra mile and offer to take them to a movie that they would like to see.

When you're driving there and a little red sports car tires to wedge in front of you, don't honk your horn and mumble expletives. Don't just tolerate the intrusion into your personal space, either. Do what you can to actually help the other driver! Back off and blink your lights to show the driver that you want to help him get in front of you. That doesn't mean you have to like a rude driver or approve of pushy behavior. But instead of being exploited, you are deliberately and willingly serving another. That puts you in charge of your own emotions and your own behavior. Not only will you and your family be safer, but you will also plant a little seed of Lasting Purpose loving and giving. The startled driver that you help just might modify his aggressive, me-first attitude and be more courteous to another driver. Like a row of dominoes, your act of love keeps multiplying and bouncing from one person to another.

When you put these principles you have learned into practice and use them for a while, giving of yourself out of an ever-larger door, and finally blowing the whole protective capsule up in the air as if you were a parachuting pilot, you will get rid of your timidity and shyness and overcome your reluctance to stand up and be the person you really want to be. You will escape from hate and fear and the certain unhappiness that such attitudes ultimately produce. That is what happens when you learn to truly live a Lasting Purpose life.

7

Keeping on Course

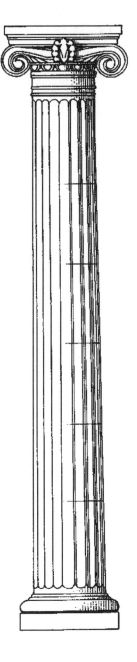

ACTING AS IF

If you are without courage, love. If you are without purpose, love. If you are without hope, love. With love as your master, you always have courage, purpose and hope. On the other hand, if you hang onto your hate and fear—as you are certainly entitled to do if that is your desire—these negative attitudes and emotions will keep you from getting out in public, attending meetings, giving speeches, and even taking a chance of initiating a friendship with another person who may be attractive (and attracted) to you. Love, on the other hand, gives you courage, makes you eager to take risks, and prods you on through setbacks and temporary disappointments.

In describing a deceased elderly friend of hers, one of the all-time great achievers, Helen Keller, wrote: "He was a man of lofty character, a man of rich spiritual gifts. His heart was pure and warm, full of childlike faith in the best he saw in his fellow-creatures, and he was always doing for other people something lovely and dear. In all his ways he kept the commandment, 'Love thy neighbor as thyself.'"

That is the description of a person living a Lasting Purpose life, giving of himself through a gigantic door. It is sad to think how few people today, in spite of their good efforts, could honestly be described in that same manner.

You, of course, can be one of the exceptions. Just keep in mind that when you first get started with your Lasting Purpose mindset of loving, serving and giving, it may feel a little uncomfortable. From time to time, your old habit of "giving to get" no doubt will try to push itself back into your Innate Subconscious Mind to guide and direct your behavior. You resist it by engaging in your loving and giving behaviors anyhow, and by speaking to yourself with complete authority, to re-establish your firm belief that you are changing into a "new and improved," happier, more peaceful, more productive person.

Speak to yourself with authority until the other part of your mind believes your affirmations of "I can, I will, I must." Then, as the conviction of "I am" comes into your mind, you can begin to just "act as if" in the proper way. That doesn't mean you become a phony and, for example, pretend you're rich when you're not. However, if you sincerely desire to adopt a new lifestyle and act as though you have done so, then the action stimulates your desire even more. In other words, once you are able to generate a vivid image of yourself being successful, if you just "pretend" you have a firm Lasting Purpose commitment, working continuously to increase your desire for its accomplishment, you will soon find that you're not pretending anymore: The state of mind you desired has become a reality. By affirming with authority that "I am," you find that you truly are.

Acting as if is a very important concept. When you can truly act as if, you are utilizing the most powerful mindset of all. You conduct yourself as though you have already achieved your goal, and you *see* yourself in the situation you desire. Acting as if creates an iron-clad mindset that is almost impossible to break.

As you keep plugging along with your acts of loving and giving under the direction of your Innate Subconscious, before you know what's happening, you'll find that you're a new person. You'll find yourself liking your new habits. You'll find that your new mindset allows you to enjoy loving, serving and giving—even if other people are throwing rocks at you. You learn that what other people think, say and do really doesn't matter. You're not controlled by what's out there.

You're controlled by what's in here—in your heart—in your Lasting Purpose mindset.

STEPPING OUT INTO THE UNKNOWN

When you are living your daily life with a Lasting Purpose mindset—loving, serving and giving out of your own abundance—you will observe an increased number of opportunities to acquire fame and fortune and the power that those entities bring with them. There is a slight complication with this phenomenon, however. Although it might seem somewhat paradoxical, you do not seek materialistic opportunities with your "giving hand," which represents that part of your mind that is bathed in Lasting Purpose love. Instead, you learn to recognize opportunities with another part of your mind in a manner that does not disturb your Lasting Purpose mindset. You can then very legitimately reach out with your "receiving hand" to earn a needed and deserved income from your time and talents. And you should do so without guilt or remorse.

No person, machine or institution can continue to exist without being fed, fueled or funded. Consider that it is only by gathering droplets of moisture from the atmosphere that a cloud is able to garner the resources necessary to produce life-giving rain. Nobody begrudges the cloud its moisture. In the same way, people who wish to live a loving, serving and giving Lasting Purpose life must also be fed, fueled and funded. This process can take many forms, but you should not try to force choices with your conscious mind.

When you have learned to talk to yourself with authority as a way to establish belief, and when you have acquired the appropriate mindset of love, the right choices will come to you from your Innate. They will come to you naturally and with very little conscious effort from you in the same way that you might experience "love at first sight." You do not plan and orchestrate such a phenomenon; it just happens. And even you, yourself, are surprised.

The same phenomenon can occur to guide you to the right career, a satisfying sport, or even a life philosophy. Your mind, however, must be made ready to receive such wisdom. Otherwise, you will be like someone trying to land a large fish without a net or gaff. The opportunity will slip out of your hands, and all you will have left is a sad story about "the one that got away."

When you go about your day being nice only to people you think can do you some good, ignoring others and sometimes even being rude to them, you can easily let the big one get away. I heard a story once about an old man dressed in over-alls who went into a Cadillac showroom many years ago and began studying the various models that were displayed on the floor. Several salesmen saw him, but they all judged him to be "just a looker," so they waited on other customers or pretended to be busy.

A young man who had just started his sales career spotted the old man, went over to him immediately, and greeted him with a sincere smile. After just a few minutes of conversation, the old man found a model he liked and wrote out a check for the whole amount. As it turned out, he was the richest farmer in a three-county area. There was no doubt about his check being good. He owned a major interest in the town's biggest bank.

If the young salesman had been as unfeeling and selective about his giving as the more experienced salesmen were, he would have missed out on an easy sale. So often people smile, bow and scrape only to the attractive, wealthy and powerful of the world, hoping to be paid for their efforts with sex, prestige, money, power or some other tangible commodity. Such behavior is without wisdom. It is never the result of internal guidance under the influence of a mindset of love. Lasting Purpose love does not discriminate.

If you are able to be still and listen to the "wee small voice" inside you, the personal relationships, career directions, areas of service and other pursuits that are right for you are, in effect, "given" to you. This guidance comes from a much wiser part of your mind, which I call the Innate Subconscious, or simply Innate.

Here, again, the magic of the formula does not require you to possess extraordinary talents and abilities. Great achievements often are made by so-called "C students" while many of the intellectually gifted seemingly waste their talents. For those with modest genetic inheritances, love and persistency can level up the playing field and make them superior competitors. The gifted, by enhancing their talents with Lasting Purpose love and persistency, can discover and conquer vast new worlds in whatever pursuits that attract them.

Whether you are strong or weak, brilliant or average, aggressive or shy, you are taken to the highest level of achievement for which you are innately suited. A person with limited academic ability would not likely become a great research scientist, of course. However, along with many of the intellectually gifted who also choose to do so, he or she may become one of the world's greatest carvers of wooden birds, a superb violinist, a very competitive truck driver, or even a world-famous chef.

The quality of your achievement is limited only by the caliber of your belief. Academic ability is not the only indication of intelligence, of course. Many people who do poorly in school are later discovered to have remarkable talents. It is interesting to note that some of the world's most creative people, including Albert Einstein and Thomas Edison, were considered to be backward by their teachers in their earlier years. People with average intellects usually think the ideas of brilliant people are "crazy" because they do not and cannot understand them.

With Lasting Purpose love, you can be successful, happy and at peace with yourself and those around you in whatever role you find yourself. You can find your niche in this world if you can find the courage to step out into the unknown and learn to let yourself be guided by the wisdom of your ever-available Innate Subconscious Mind. This in itself is quite an accomplishment.

Many people seem to react to whatever environment in which they find themselves as though they were baby birds imprisoned in their nest. In their frustration with their limited world, they flop and squawk and stretch over the edge, sometimes falling out before they're mature enough to fly. Toddlers can't wait to be "big kids"; teenagers struggle to get away from home and parental control; and most working people are constantly looking for a way to get away from their job to a mythical "something better."

In reality, most of the time the "something better" is right here, right now, in this place in time and space. The real challenge is to learn how to reach into your own mind and find it. Many people have gone through life hopping from one job to another only to discover, through mature reflection, that they would have been better off staying with their first position. The same is true with mates, investments, houses, hobbies, etc. The grass rarely is actually greener on the other side of the fence. To cows, baby birds and me-first people, it just looks that way.

CONNECTING THE DOTS

Learning to utilize a mindset to become totally and irreversibly focused and committed is one of the major concepts of Lasting Purpose. It is through the use of the Lasting Purpose mindset that you are able to stabilize your personality, fortifying and developing winning ways about you that attract people to you and help pave the way to achievement.

When you develop a Lasting Purpose mindset, it's not necessary to be able to consciously and continuously visualize the end product of your dream, as long as love is involved. Once the big picture is firmly implanted in your Innate Subconscious Mind, taking it one step at a time as directed by your Innate Subconscious is all you need to do. Typically, you are shown by the Innate how to establish the next contact while you're on the road to your accomplishment.

We have all seen the "connect the dots" drawings in children's coloring books. In the same way that a child connects these with a pencil line to make a picture, in an Innate-directed life you continue to move from one event to the next successive event, not worrying about the big picture that will be revealed by the final connection. Of course, the big picture is always in the back of your mind. You have talked to yourself with authority, generated the belief and implanted the vision. Nothing will deter you. One straight line of activity may seem to have no significance, but you are confident that the final product will be there as opportunities and road markers are given to you all along the way. All you have to do is trustingly follow them without a lot of conscious-minded censorship, doubt and fear.

Later, as you begin to make things happen with love, you are able to create and expand the necessary work plans to get the job done. Even if you are temporarily beaten (which will happen along the way from time to time), as long as you stay in the game, you will be given other opportunities to get back on the right road—and sometimes it's a higher and better road than the one you were on before. You might be jilted by one person, only to turn right around and find the true love of your life. You might get fired from a mediocre job and, forced to start your own business, become a millionaire.

You have to ditch your conscious pride, of course, and, if you choose to play, pay the price of success at the re-entry toll gate, whatever that price might be. For Thomas Edison, it was thousands of experiment failures. For Abraham Lincoln, it was numerous political defeats. For B.J. Palmer, it was constant derision and rejection by the so-called "scientific community." For me, it was first broken bones on the football field, then (as you will soon see) several burned-out buildings and many bloody battles with the entrenched powers, all in the name of chiropractic.

For you, too, the price may be repeated failures, rejections and heartaches. As long as you have love and persistency, however, you are never defeated; you are only momentarily detained.

As you proceed forward with unshakable authority, your intense internal desire keeps the avenues and channels to and from the Innate Subconscious Mind open to your educated, consciously-directed mind. You are given what you need to be a winner. You will soon be able to say, "I am! I am a winner!" And you will simply be describing the reality that is.

8

The Yin and Yang of Living in Harmony

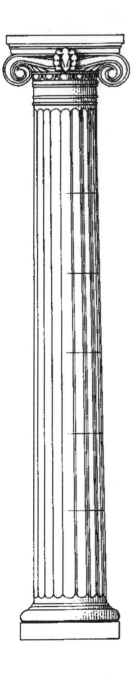

GOING BEYOND INTUITION

Throughout my life, I have searched for the most efficient and satisfying way to get a job done. Whether I was learning to throw a knife, playing football, selling cookware, or promoting and defending the great profession of chiropractic, doing things "the way they've always been done" was of no interest to me. I wanted to cut new paths and blaze new trails and to do things in a way that would lead to success consistently and dependably.

In searching for the magic formula for success, I looked to writings of the world's geniuses, both ancient and modern. More important, however, I looked into the depths of my own Innate Subconscious Mind. I put questions to the "genius within" that is available to every person who is able to persist and develop the firm belief that the answer is waiting within and wants to be discovered.

As time passed and I continued to take one step after another that led to a higher understanding of the innate mysteries of the human mind, I finally found myself with a chest full of tools available for my use anytime I needed them. As I shared these principles with fellow professionals through Dynamic Essentials lectures and other discourses, it became increasingly clear that these were principles that could be learned by anyone with a quick wit and a spirit of adventure.

What I am now able to share with you, as you have seen in previous pages, is a revolutionary new way of accessing and utilizing the super-dynamic potential of the Innate Subconscious Mind. You learn to encourage yourself through the positive affirmations of "I can, I will, I must," talking to yourself with authority until you develop a strong and enduring belief. That belief then helps generate a vision of what you want to achieve, and that vision, in turn, accesses your Innate Subconscious Mind and puts it to work for you.

When this dynamic technique of "speaking and living with authority" is coupled with the principles of Lasting Purpose, meaning you persistently love, serve and give out of your own abundance, just for the sake of doing it, the unique combination puts you light years ahead of your competition in developing helpful long-term relationships and achieving your worthy goals and objectives. Once you develop the Lasting Purpose mindset, it quiets and overcomes your conscious, educated mind, which then allows thought flashes to come through and light the best pathway to reach your objective. In time, you may even get a persistent stream of thought flashes that provide direction for your whole life moment by moment. Such an experience greatly enhances your overall productivity and enjoyment of life.

The principles of Lasting Purpose and living with authority go far beyond what is rather simplistically referred to as intuition, although I use that term from time to time to refer to the source of thought flashes. The fact is, however, that intuition is to the total system that has evolved in my life what a little arc of static electricity is to a bolt of lightning. There's just no comparison.

The Lasting Purpose life lived with authority brings with it not only huge opportunities, but also tremendous responsibilities. When you fully and completely commit to a Lasting Purpose lifestyle, you quickly develop the ability to influence large numbers of people. You then also inherit the responsibility and obligation to use that Lasting Purpose influence wisely and compassionately. When you fail to do so, the same abuse that you heap upon others often comes back on you, multiplied many times. We have all witnessed many great and promising talents lured into that dead-end trap of selfishness and exploitation of others, as their egos rise and drive them to ruin. World-class athletes go to prison, tycoons go broke and kill themselves, and military dictators are mutilated in the streets by the people they once ruled.

The dreams that you develop as you live a Lasting Purpose life may seem quite outlandish and unachievable to many of your friends and relatives, and in reality, you may see 10, 20 or even 30 years or more pass before you are given the opportunity to put your plans into action. The major difference between you, as a Lasting Purpose practitioner, and others is that when the opportunity finally does present itself, you are ready! You keep your lamp filled and your wick trimmed. If opportunity knocks in the middle of the night, you open the door and usher it in.

Sometimes the doors of opportunity just swing wide open for you; at other times, you may have to take the initiative and kick them open. Nevertheless, with another non-conflicting part of your mind, you are always sensitive to such materialistic opportunities, and you reach out for them with "your other hand."

I'm not talking about some kind of schizophrenic personality division, of course. The natural phenomenon I am referring to here is the same as when you find yourself in a wonderfully euphoric mood as you're taking off for a vacation along an uncluttered highway while you listen to a favorite tune on the radio and plan what you are going to do when you get to your destination. These different functions require a very delicate cognitive balance. A harsh, blaring commercial on the radio, for example, can be very distracting and interfere with your conscious planning activities. A near-accident can divert all your attention to the steering wheel and the brakes of your car. Negative thoughts about the cost of your vacation and overdue credit card bills can block your enjoyment of the music as well as your ability to drive safely.

However, with a mindset of Lasting Purpose love, you can continue to balance all three mental activities and do each one of them well. Your driving hand does not interfere with your music enjoyment hand, and neither of them impinges upon the cognitive processes relating to your planning activities. They all work in harmony, each respectful of the space and boundaries of the others.

FINDING TRUE WEALTH

Many people go about their daily lives with such intense concentration on the materialistic requisites of life that they all but totally ignore the spiritual enlightenment and enhancement that come from within. Like children who cling to the bank of a stream, fearful of risking more than getting their toes wet, these people are afraid to venture out into the bold innate stream of life. They look out with envy as they see others joyfully bathing in the wisdom and opportunities that an innate-directed life can offer, but they will not let go of their conscious-minded control. Learning to live the Lasting Purpose life is like learning to swim. With a burning desire to swim and an absolute belief that you can, you will and you must swim, you jump into the water and persistently pursue the vision that tells you that you are swimming.

People who will not let go of the security of the bank are afraid to reach out for greater horizons. They choose to continue to plug along on dead-end jobs just to pay the rent and bring home a few groceries, never daring to listen to the pleading voice coming from their Innate Subconscious Mind that says, "Follow your dream! Choose to do it! Choose to take a chance!"

All civilized societies need dependable, responsible people to do the jobs required to hold its fabric together, of course. And I am not suggesting that everybody should quit his job, desert family and go off treasure hunting. I am suggesting, however, that a person who is without a dream and hope of achieving that dream is spiritually dead. To fail to pursue your noble love is to murder the soul. A simple farmer lovingly tending his crops and truly enjoying every day of his life to the fullest is much more evolved as a human being than is a "wealthy" corporate lawyer who has to sniff cocaine to make his daily life bearable.

Fortunately, a great number of us are able to keep one hand on the plow of civilized responsibility while also reaching out to the stars with the other. Such a balance becomes much easier once you reach inside yourself and tap into the great wisdom that is always accessible there. That's what Lasting Purpose lived with authority is all about. It provides you with the tools to organize and harmoniously integrate your life for maximum production and minimum stress. You are able to enjoy and share your natural talents and interests while, at the same time, you are constantly and consistently ready for whatever challenge or opportunity for improvement in your life that might come your way.

The Lasting Purpose habit continues to build an internal fortress of love, and then materialistic achievements and success can take their rightful place. Lasting Purpose love is never allowed to be dominated by selfish and purely materialistic ambitions, however. Love must always be your master and the primary motivating force in all situations in which you find yourself.

To use our happy vacationer metaphor again, your first priority has to be to drive the car safely. Enjoying music and making plans are always secondary. You can do without the music and make your plans later, but if the car crashes and kills you, the music and your plans die with you. The same is true with Lasting Purpose love and persistency. If you reach out too greedily with your receiving hand and let loving, serving and giving crash, then your receiving activities will shortly crash and come to an end, too. Many are the professionals, businesspeople and politicians who have made this discovery the hard way.

One question I am often asked is, "Will Lasting Purpose guarantee you material riches?" If that is truly your heart's desire, then it certainly is possible to achieve it with a Lasting Purpose mindset. Once you discover and claim a project that you can see completed in your mind's eye, and you really believe that you can achieve it, then you can acquire wealth through the sale of beneficial and marketable services, products or ideas. Certainly the success trinity of Lasting Purpose love, persistency and talking with authority to establish belief can give you the ability to achieve at any level. Your only limitations are your own natural ability, your desire and your willingness to pay the price for success.

Wealth itself, of course, cannot buy happiness, and it may not even be a good thing for you to have great material wealth. For some people, a huge sum of money would be a curse. The modern multi-million-dollar lotteries have demonstrated that fact time and again. Many people have had their lives ruined with sudden wealth for which they were not mentally and spiritually prepared. Some rags-to-riches celebrities also have found the challenge of their sudden wealth and power to be too much for them to handle. Being a child movie star has shown itself to be an especially hazardous profession. If you acquire a Lasting Purpose mindset first, however, you can deal with whatever challenge life has to offer.

Although not everybody can be rich, I am confident that it is intended for each of us to be happy and at peace with ourselves and the universe. The real ingredients of enduring peace and happiness are available to everyone. Whether prince or pauper, if love is your master, you will always have the opportunity to experience joy.

Some people spend their whole lives lamenting the lot they have been given in life. They may think of themselves as too homely, too shy, too dull-witted or too poorly educated to ever "acquire" true happiness. The only deficits that will guarantee you failure and unhappiness, however, are a lack of love, focus, persistency and the ability to speak to yourself with authority, the latter of which produces absolute belief and a burning vision in your mind's eye. Without these magic ingredients, you are like a satellite lost in space without the power to alter your course. With them, you have an anchor and a directional force. With faith and belief, you can create a vision within your inner eye. And whatever you can perceive and believe will come to pass if you work lovingly and persistently to achieve your vision.

Whether we achieve happiness is determined not so much by the path destiny has given us to travel, but by the style, confidence, innate intelligence and authority with which we walk that path. Whether you have many material possessions or few, Lasting Purpose love enables you to possess the great wealth of internal peace and harmony with the universe.

When you penetrate to the potential wisdom of the Innate Subconscious Mind, all people, in a sense, are created equal. Everybody has an Innate. Through Lasting Purpose, you can choose to achieve the level of material prosperity and spiritual actualization that is innately possible and right for you wherever you are in the world. If you are fortunate enough to be in the United States of America, you have the greatest opportunity for achievement because you have the most freedom to alter and change your directions.

As most happy people have learned, happiness comes not from what you receive, nor even from what you have to give; rather, it comes from what you have remaining in your heart when you have given freely out of your own abundance.

IT'S OKAY TO FEED THE GOOSE

Whether you're the president of a giant corporation, running your own small business, working for wages, taking care of a home and family or already retired, the same law of return governs your life and what you get from it. You might run a big company for years with a "small-door" focus and point proudly every year to your profit statement as verification that what you are doing is right. But you would do well to ask yourself if this has brought happiness into your life. If it has, great! Keep on your course. If you are not experiencing happiness, however, and you're feeling a huge void in your life even though you have all the material trappings of success, then you need to consider the merits of adding Lasting Purpose to your life. You can continue with your successful enterprises, but you need to also begin giving through a bigger door—loving, serving and giving out of your own abundance. This strategy will add true and enduring internal happiness while also greatly enhancing your material success.

Lasting Purpose does not demand that you give away all the material possessions that you have. There is nothing wrong with feeding the goose that lays the golden eggs. It is perfectly moral and ethical to achieve material success while you're living a Lasting Purpose commitment. Some outstandingly good people who constantly and continuously bless the world with their Lasting Purpose type of giving of themselves seem to be repulsed by the prospect of personal material gain. If being of modest means makes them happy, it is their right to avoid the accumulation of wealth. Wealth, after all, is a relative state of being. In some places in the world, you are considered relatively poor if you have only one new car; in other places, you are rich if you own one donkey.

Rich or poor, you can still live a Lasting Purpose life. If, however, you feel you can be more effective with wealth, as productive ideas filter down to you, you can respond to them with love and begin to organize a plan of action—with generosity and compassion for others, always continuing to love, serve and give.

Very few people in the world save very much of the money they earn. Most are eager to spend it. They spend it as soon as they get it, and often for foolish things. If you have a product, idea or service of value, people will be happy to give you their money in exchange for it. All you have to do is offer it in a manner compatible with the principles of Lasting Purpose and then be ready to count your money. It will come.

You must be constantly alert, however, to avoid forsaking your Lasting Purpose commitment. It's as though there are two parts of you—two separate personalities—and while the two must work together in harmony like yin and yang, the giving hand does not have to know what the getting hand is doing. In that way, you can continue to build great enterprises while, in the quiet recesses of your mind, you continue to give of yourself through a big door. That has been the method of success for thousands of entrepreneurs who have made tremendous contributions to the good of humankind. They are the ones who do not have to set up foundations of apology when they get old. Even with their wealth, they have lived saintly lives. The world would be a sad place, indeed, if we permitted only negative, self-serving individuals to become wealthy.

9

Lasting Purpose and Chiropractic

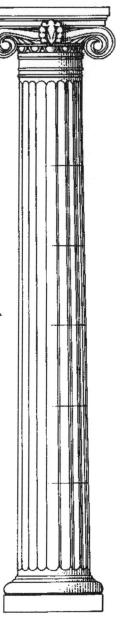

PAYING THE PRICE

While holding the part-time sales positions with Electrolux and WearEver, my young bride and I worked our way through college to receive our Doctor of Chiropractic degrees in 1956. As newly graduated doctors, we set up our first practice in Austell, Georgia, a small suburb of Atlanta. With total belief in chiropractic and a fervent dedication to our "magnificent obsession" to educate the world about the staggering potential of this young healing science, Dr. Nell and I began to make ourselves known.

Fulfilling our vision, in about five years our practice had expanded to a total of 19 clinics throughout the Southeast. This included seven clinics in African-American communities in Atlanta called the Triple H Chiropractic Health Centers. The three H's represented "Health, Harmony and Happiness." Building our practice on the policy that everyone should be treated with love and compassion in a professional manner, and that no one should be denied chiropractic care because of an inability to pay, our business flourished. The compassionate philosophy that enabled us to develop our business was well on its way to gaining international recognition.

But as you know, the materialistic world is not always receptive to those guided by unselfish compassion. This was made clear to me when, because of our unpopular effort to help people in what was then acceptably called the "colored community," Dr. Nell and I were denied memberships in the Christian Chiropractic Association. The Georgia Board of Chiropractic Examiners even tried, without success, to revoke my professional license in 1958 for daring to advertise by using the mailing pieces I had purchased from the Palmer College of Chiropractic. The real issue that some chiropractors found so threatening, however, was that Dr. Nell and I were offering our services on the basis of love and human need rather than on an inflexible fee system that would have turned some patients away.

I continued to generate controversy by my dedication to traditional chiropractic, my promotion of the rights of the sick to choose the doctor and method of their choice, and my insistence upon serving all people equally, regardless of their ability to pay. As a result, our $500,000 shopping center in the Austell-Lithia Springs area that contained our Chiropractic Health Center was mysteriously burned to the ground—twice, on dates exactly one year apart.

There was still work to be done, however. As I continued to maintain a Lasting Purpose mindset, I became increasingly sensitive to the needs of the growing chiropractic community for creative, well-written informational brochures and pamphlets for patients. This inspired the founding of Si-Nel Publishing. The Si-Nel Publishing facilities were also totally destroyed by a mysterious fire.

Discouraged but not beaten, Dr. Nell and I fought doggedly on to keep the spirit of B.J. Palmer's chiropractic alive. A major thrust of this battle was resisting the 1960 attempted merger and ultimate destruction of the International Chiropractors Association, which was founded by Dr. B.J. Palmer himself. In spite of the financial costs and sacrifices required of my family, it never occurred to me to do anything but remain true to my beliefs, convinced that the principles that would preserve chiropractic for the multitudes were more important than material comforts and personal profits.

Buoyed by the continuing success of Life Dynamic Essentials Seminars, in 1966 Dr. Nell and I founded the Life Foundation, which is now an IRS-approved, 501(c)3, non-profit chiropractic organization dedicated to the purpose of service, education and research. One of the many successful projects generated by this enterprise was Health for Life, a tabloid newspaper distributed by chiropractors and read by millions of patients.

In addition to publishing educational materials, the Life Foundation established the Health Mobile, a modern, completely equipped chiropractic clinic-on-wheels. This free-service program introduced chiropractic to thousands of people in the U.S. as it traveled from state to state. Later on, the self-contained facility was utilized as a health clinic that provided chiropractic care for people in an impoverished area of Atlanta. The Life Foundation eventually purchased a single piece of depressed property in downtown Atlanta to establish a permanent chiropractic clinic staffed by personnel from Life Chiropractic College. Today, the Life Foundation Atlanta clinic holdings have expanded to three-quarters of a city block.

Throughout the earlier part of my professional career, I continued to be encouraged in my efforts on behalf of the profession by a number of treasured recognitions. The Georgia Chiropractic Association, for example, voted me Chiropractor of the Year in 1972 in recognition of my accomplishments as their representative at the State Legislature for over a decade. This was an especially big honor for a person with my humble beginning, but there was still much work to do. And, equipped with a Lasting Purpose mindset, I was ready to do my part and then some.

To counter the American Medical Association's political success in excluding chiropractic from participation in Medicare, I launched a campaign that resulted in more than two million letters being written by chiropractic patients and other supporters to their Congressmen. As a result, in July

1973 a landmark decision was handed down to include chiropractic services in this major federal health care program.

Three years later, another landmark case, Wilk vs. American Medical Association, began. The Wilk case was an antitrust suit in which the American Medical Association was accused of engaging in an illegal conspiracy to contain and eliminate chiropractic. Several Dynamic Essentials friends and I had already instituted our own suit as a federal civil rights case to protect chiropractors from discrimination. Recognizing the potential broad significance of the Wilk case, however, and seeing that it was more firmly grounded, I urged the Scientific Civil Rights Foundation to drop its suit. For the next seven years, we all worked unrelentingly in support of the Wilk case and the chiropractic profession.

Finally, on August 27, 1987, the U.S. District Court in Chicago ruled in favor of chiropractors. In a 101-page opinion, the court found that the AMA and its members participated in a conspiracy against chiropractors in violation of the nation's antitrust laws. The AMA was permanently enjoined from restricting its members from professionally associating with chiropractors or engaging in other anti-competitive acts. This fervently fought order was a bitter pill for the AMA to swallow because it greatly enhanced the status and competitiveness of chiropractic. It was a sweet victory for chiropractors and their patients everywhere.

I also found myself being thrust into the leadership of many demonstrations for chiropractic licensure in the various unlicensed states. The most significant one was in Baton Rouge, Louisiana, where over 500 marchers converged on the State Capitol to demand chiropractic licensure and freedom of choice. Along with the Louisiana supporters, we organized a large mock Cajun funeral where "People's Rights" were buried.

A casket was carried by the demonstrators from the center of Baton Rouge to the State Capitol, the participants all dressed in black and the women in their mourning veils. I still vividly recall being confronted on the Capitol steps by none other than the chairman of the AMA's Committee on Quackery himself, Dr. J.A. Sabatier. He had the door to the main entrance of the State Capitol blocked.

This was not the beginning of the AMA's crusade against chiropractic, and it would not be the end. For the past 100 years, the greater our success in bringing better health to our patients has been, and the more we are acclaimed by the general public, the more vicious the campaign becomes. If, as the old American Indian custom has it, it is an honor to have powerful enemies, then the chiropractic profession is honored indeed. I continued to feel compelled, however, to keep that honor within tolerable limits.

THE BEGINNING OF LIFE

For many years in my lecture series, I shared my dream of seeing a chiropractic college established in rapidly growing metropolitan Atlanta. Such an institution would be founded upon the guiding principles of Lasting Purpose and would be the logical extension of the education, research and service efforts already being promoted by the Life Foundation. Knowing the folly of rushing a dream, however, I continued with the job at hand of providing leadership where it was needed, assured that through inner guidance, I would find the answer within me as to the right time and place to start this important mission. I was also confident that the means to make the vision I saw in my mind's eye a reality would be provided.

From the beginning, as I continued to speak to myself with authority, the thought flashes provided by my Innate Subconscious Mind caused me to envision a college founded on the separate and distinct principles of chiropractic that had been established under the law in various states. I gradually developed an obsession to see a college accredited by all official government accrediting agencies, so that graduates would never be questioned about the reliability of their academic credentials. The graduates of the college would be equipped to disseminate universal truths about life and health discovered through chiropractic, ably standing shoulder to shoulder with other learned professionals and generating increasing acceptance and recognition for the chiropractic profession. In a message to my fellow chiropractors about building a new chiropractic college, I wrote: "The purpose of Life Chiropractic College will be to train young people from all walks of life . . . not only to become skilled doctors of chiropractic, but also to become meaningful human beings whose innate goodness will touch and affect all who come in contact with them."

As I had known would happen one day, in 1974 the time came for the college I had been visualizing all these years to become a reality. With the help of Dr. Nell, my tireless and talented mate, and with generous assistance from dedicated people like Dr. D. D. Humber—whose loyalty, encouragement and willingness to believe in my vision provided a sanctuary of support—our greatest project ever was begun. With an army of friends and supporters of Dynamic Essentials and chiropractic behind us, Life Chiropractic College (now Life College) was chartered in September 1974. Even though the resources were meager, a board of trustees was appointed and the dream took a small but significant first step forward toward becoming a reality.

When Life Chiropractic College first opened its doors on January 20, 1975, 22 students enrolled for classes held in makeshift classrooms. These stalwart students became known as the "Day One Class." Since that modest but determined beginning, enrollment in the D.C. program alone has swelled to over 3,200 students, making it the largest school of chiropractic in the world. In 1995, the combined student body of chiropractic, undergraduate and graduate students totaled over 4,000, representing 47 states and 33 other countries, served by over 600 faculty and staff.

Over the years, I have seen Life College gain international recognition for its activities relating to such events as the 1986 Goodwill Games and the Life Around the World (LAW) Program, which is co-sponsored by the Life Foundation. This program's purpose is to introduce chiropractic health care to as many governments as possible, so that people around the world will have knowledge of and access to the benefits of chiropractic. Auxiliary research and service programs have also been established in a number of countries in conjunction with local universities and hospitals. Life College also has been identified by the World Health Organization as a collaborating center for its lower-back pain study. That project is ongoing, with research projects being conducted in Egypt and in Marietta, Georgia—and soon to be in Brazil, Malaysia and Russia.

Life College continues to grow, and I see many achievements in our future. Our goal is to love, serve and give out of our own abundance. We are always pleased, of course, if our efforts cause others to think of us as being worthy of honor. As with a good student, while we are not working "just for the grade," maintaining an "A" average helps to tell us when we're doing the job right.

LIVING THE DREAM

Looking back at the past 100 years of the steady upward climb of chiropractic, and looking ahead to the opportunities of the 21st century, I have a vision of an ever-expanding role for chiropractic in meeting the challenge of health care for the world. With a burning desire to be a part of this magnificent vision, I am currently involved in a number of projects that will demonstrate chiropractic's broad applications both in preventing disease and restoring health. A comprehensive textbook, *Chiropractic: Its Science and Philosophy,* written for both the lay person and the professional, is nearing completion. Other books already completed include *Looking Back to See Ahead,* an everyday resource manual, and *The Dynamic Essentials of Office Procedures and Patient Management,* which has become a standard in Dynamic Essentials seminars and a textbook for thousands of chiropractors.

Also in development are plans for a television outreach for chiropractic, which will be beamed from the Life College campus to people throughout the world via satellite. Under the banner of this Healthy Living Network, people of all ages and socioeconomic classes around the world will be taught how to enhance wellness through proper spinal hygiene, diet, exercise and living by the principles of Lasting Purpose. Another related project being perfected is a nationwide television program designed to encourage senior citizens and others to seek chiropractic care as a way to improve the quality of their lives.

From early on in my professional career, it became and remained my purpose to carry on, enhance and validate the noble traditions of the new science begun by the developers of chiropractic, Drs. D.D. and B.J. Palmer. Tenacious dedication to the principles of pure chiropractic continues to earn me a treasured position of leadership and recognition as one of the major defenders and protectors of this health care profession, which, even at 100 years old, is still relatively young.

I believe the application of this basic Lasting Purpose philosophy to other walks of life is just as valid as it is with chiropractic. Adopting a Lasting Purpose mindset helps you to be a better parent and a better mate, a better citizen, a better employer and employee, a better entrepreneur and a better person in anything you choose to do. It is therefore my intention to offer an expanded version of Dynamic Essentials worldwide to non-chiropractic business and professional audiences as well. With the understanding you will have gained from this book, you may very well want to be one of our first students!

10

Lasting Power

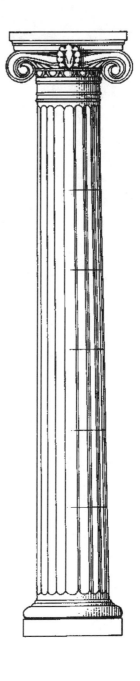

THE POWER OF PURPOSE

As you have seen in the preceding pages, the Lasting Purpose formula of love, compassion, desire, persistency and focus enabled me to not only sell myself, but also to sell chiropractic as a legitimate and deserving health care profession. Whenever I needed it, the almost mystical power produced by a Lasting Purpose mindset was there. It was there to help me learn the science of chiropractic and to do my part in advancing my profession. It was there to help me successfully fight the many powerful enemies of true chiropractic. It was there to provide the inspiration and means for taking 22 students and a rented warehouse and founding what is now the world's largest chiropractic college.

Lasting Purpose continues to work for me and others each and every time its great resources are called upon. It can also work for you. The world needs dreamers, but even more, it needs dreamers who know how to turn their vision into reality. By adopting the principles you learn from this book, you can be one of those much-needed achievers.

I hope that these words, shared with you in the spirit of loving, serving and giving, have stimulated your interest in the philosophy that built Life College. Even more, I hope they helped clarify and provide focus for your own goals and beliefs. As you begin to apply the principles you have learned to your own life, you are certain to gain further insights into the secrets of the wisdom and power of Lasting Purpose. Once the seed is planted with authority in fertile ground, your own Innate will take it, add to it, and grow it to fulfill your own particular needs. Like the forces of nature, the power of Lasting Purpose is unlimited. All who put up their windmills or sails, whether small or large, can partake of the power of the wind. The same is true of Lasting Purpose.

SETTING THE JOURNEY IN MOTION

A final thought: once you turn over a new leaf—which is just another way of saying that you abandon the focus of one mindset and take on another, better one—you should not be disappointed if an immediate payoff is not forthcoming. Good things will begin to happen in your life once you've made the Lasting Purpose commitment. When you are talking to yourself with authority, and when you can see the vision and believe what you see, then almost irrevocable events are set in motion. It's like pushing the first little rock that starts a giant avalanche. Your Innate Subconscious Mind is working; the creativity is there. Just be patient.

Give other people time to recognize and accept the new, more loving, serving and giving you. It sometimes takes people a while to catch up with your rapid paradigm shifts. Just enjoy the increased peace and harmony in your life as you love, serve and give out of your own abundance, doing it just for the sake of doing it. When you turn around, eventually those around you will turn around, too, and accept you for what you really are instead of what you once were.

Realize, of course, that all the time you are practicing Lasting Purpose and living your life with authority, you are building up a priceless reserve of love and persistency that will make the path you have chosen in life ever brighter and more satisfying. Even if you find yourself sometimes without material resources, you still will never be poor.

That does not mean you'll never encounter an obstacle or that everybody you meet will roll out the red carpet of welcome for you. Some very negative people tend to hate positive-minded, loving "do-gooders" and do everything possible to try to destroy them. Regardless of what the few do to you, in the long run, the law of just returns will work in your favor. Sooner or later, you'll get what you have earned and deserve.

I wish you well and thank you for allowing me to love, serve and give by sharing my life and philosophy of life with you through this book. As you put Lasting Purpose into practice, I hope and trust you will share your joy with others. I would also enjoy hearing of your successes.

As you go about your travels in life with a Lasting Purpose mindset, there will be many occasions for celebration. At such times, as you achieve a little victory with the help of Lasting Purpose, I would be pleased if you remembered this visit with me and whispered to yourself, "Press hard—there are three copies!"

In the meantime, I wish you a happy and prosperous journey.

Appendix

MAPPING THE JOURNEY TO LASTING PURPOSE: A GUIDE TO KEY TERMS

As you pursue your journey of Lasting Purpose, you may on occasion need to pause and revisit some of the "high points" you encountered along the way. In this section, you will find a description of those "places"—the terms and phrases used throughout the book to define the path of Lasting Purpose.

GIVING THROUGH A BIG DOOR

With a Lasting Purpose mindset, you practice "giving through a big door." You put no limits on your giving of kindness, support, appreciation, recognition of merit, etc. By giving freely of yourself, the natural law of just returns is activated to bring back to you many times what you give.

LOVE

"Love," in the Lasting Purpose philosophy, refers to an attitude more than an emotion. By maintaining a mindset of love, you can always deal compassionately and effectively with other human beings. This mindset of *agape* love does not require you to actually love or even like a particular individual in a personal or physical sense. This love reaches out beyond any personal judgments you may have and loves through you, as you "let it reach out to all beings and all things in all ways."

When you allow love to love through you, you are engaging in positive, compassionate acts without discrimination and without imposing conscious negative judgments upon the love's purity. You are not necessarily loving with your conscious, educated mind. You are allowing the huge abundance of agape love that comes from and through your Innate Subconscious Mind to express itself through you.

As you allow love to love through you, you also are allowing love to be your master. You do not allow attitudes or actions to interfere with your commitment to love, serve and give out of your own abundance just for the sake of doing so. Everything about you is caring and compassionate, including your looks, words and mannerisms, how you touch people, and so forth. This is a necessary first step in learning to enjoy the Lasting Purpose life.

DIVINE LATITUDE

Once you learn to maintain an attitude dominated by *agape* love, the state of consciousness called "divine latitude" can be achieved. This is a very peaceful state of mind in which love is your master and the typical negative bombardments of hate, fear, envy and jealousy are not accepted by your mind for prolonged periods of time.

A good way to understand divine latitude is to imagine yourself floating down a peaceful stream of love that flows from your Innate Subconscious Mind. On one side of the stream is a high cliff full of jagged rocks ready to tumble down in an avalanche with the slightest provocation. On the other side, you see a steaming swamp filled with mud and quicksand. These barriers represent the negative thoughts that can distract you from your course and present a barrier to your success. In the swamp, you might find thoughts based on greed, envy, jealousy and hate. On the rocky side, you might be distracted by lust, selfish ambition and self-centeredness. You can be drowned on one side or crushed on the other if you lose that very fragile, precious balance that comes only from staying the course straight down the middle of the stream.

Achieving the divine latitude is a necessary first step to being in the flow for any sustained period of time. When you are in the flow, love is persistently flowing out of your own abundance as you think and behave in a compassionate manner, as guided by your Innate Subconscious Mind. You remain in constant communication with your Innate Subconscious Mind; your creativity and productivity are maximized.

GIVING AND RECEIVING

I sometimes speak of "the other hand" and "another part of your mind" when discussing the delicate balance that must be maintained between spiritual and temporal activities. When you are attempting to sustain a Lasting Purpose mindset of loving, serving and giving and, at the same time, seek just compensation for your ideas, products and services, you attend to this latter activity with your receiving hand. Each activity must be mentally distanced from the other.

With a Lasting Purpose mindset, giving just to get is never the conscious goal of your behavior. You learn to do just for the sake of doing, meaning you enjoy the work itself and the opportunity to use the work to practice love and persistency for their own sake. In this process, of course, the practitioner of Lasting Purpose usually encounters many opportunities to benefit in material ways, if that is his or her desire. Such material achievements, however, are never allowed to be the primary driving force in one's life.

INNATE SUBCONSCIOUS MIND

"Innate" is an often-used term that goes beyond the simple dictionary definition of "inborn" or "hereditary." When used as a short version of Innate Subconscious Mind, it denotes the God within, which is sometimes also referred to as the warrior within. Innate, in this broader sense, is represented by the thought flash or a persuasive, all-knowing directional signal that is coming directly from the infinite wisdom of the Innate Subconscious Mind.

Most classical religions, including Christianity, acknowledge in some way that "the Kingdom of Heaven" is inside us. It is this bit of Universal Intelligence inside all human beings that allows individuals to communicate with one another in a "sixth-sense" manner.

By expanding Dr. B.J. Palmer's term of "Innate" to "Innate Subconscious Mind" and giving it a more definite operational meaning, I was able to gain new insight into the functioning of my mind. In the text, the terms Innate, Innate Subconscious Mind and Innate Subconscious are sometimes used interchangeably, but Innate Subconscious Mind should always be understood. The Innate Subconscious Mind is that part of the subconscious mind that generates verbalized thoughts and ideas in the mind. The part of human intelligence to which it refers is far above and beyond common conscious-minded intelligence.

"Innate," as used by B.J. Palmer, referred to the innate ability of the body to govern and manage all the primary functions of the tissue cells. He also used it as this eruption of the mind when it gives you ideas, thoughts and formal thought flashes that are not audible but still are clearly defined. They might come in the form of pictures or in words.

The Innate Subconscious Mind refers specifically to this source of humans' native intelligence, resourcefulness and creativity that can be continuously available to the trained individual. Palmer's "Innate" guides all cellular functioning of the body and provides "thot flashes," as he termed them, in response to formally stated needs. The Innate Subconscious Mind, on the other hand, also knows how to take care of an individual in his daily life, guiding him with infinite wisdom moment by moment.

The Innate Subconscious Mind provides more than just thought flashes. It enables an individual to achieve a peaceful transcendent state of being that is the equivalent of "praying without ceasing." In this euphoric state, every thought is a thought flash—a communication from Universal Intelligence.

The Innate Subconscious Mind, through Universal Intelligence (the mind of God), provides a communications link with all other forms of life through their own respective innate resources. Just as most people would agree that there is only one Universal Intelligence, so is there only one Innate or Innate Subconscious Mind. In the same way that everyone on earth breathes the same atmosphere and every fish in the ocean breathes the same ocean, so does every person's Innate spring from and connect to the same greater body of Universal Intelligence.

CONSCIOUS/EDUCATED MIND

The terms "conscious mind" and "educated mind" are used interchangeably. They refer to that part of our thinking apparatus that is very physical, worldly and limited in scope, as opposed to the more spiritual and expansive nature of the Innate Subconscious Mind. People who depend wholly upon the logical, rational, educated intelligence of their conscious mind tend to be lacking in imagination, creativity and daring. They fear and distrust any wisdom from the Innate Subconscious Mind, which is the source of "the wee small voice within."

WEE SMALL VOICE WITHIN

The "wee small voice within" can be given a variety of interpretations, depending upon your religious leanings. As I use it, it typically means the strong private thoughts that are generated by the Innate Subconscious Mind. I assume that the wee small voice is the voice of Universal Intelligence, or God, talking to me. Whatever your interpretation, when you have learned to identify and pay attention to this voice, you will find it to be a continuous source of great comfort and wisdom. It is through such an innate connection that we are able to experience thought flashes.

THOUGHT FLASH

A "thought flash" is creative intelligence in capsule form that just suddenly pops into your conscious mind, seemingly "out of the blue." The thought flash sometimes is poetically referred to as "an inspiration from the gods." The information contained in thought flashes often seems to contradict your rational, conscious-minded intelligence and, indeed, appears to go beyond the education and knowledge of the recipient. It's as though thought flashes were a direct communication from a source much wiser than your conscious mind. Often, it is only when the communications are accepted and acted upon, in spite of resistance by the conscious mind, that their true value can be realized.

Thought flashes have been a commonly reported occurrence throughout history. No doubt, a thought flash led early humans to begin using a fire to warm their camp and cook their food. Other thought flashes led humans to "invent" knives, spears, bows and arrows, guns, rockets and nuclear bombs. Every great invention is first a vision, usually followed by thought flashes that expand the vision into a reality.

When interpreted correctly, the thought flash actually gives you the opportunity to know God's will for you at that moment, or in some event, or for some directional change. In a sense, as you seek to follow and express God's will, you will want to have a constant, innate connection with God. If engaged in this innate flow, you are not seeking to have God do your will, but to know and do God's will.

A thought flash is a communication that filters up from deep within the Innate Subconscious Mind, like a bubble slowly rising from the bottom of a pond. It is only when the bubble reaches the surface that the conscious mind begins to perceive and understand it. Understanding often comes in several stages, with the final stage being the achievement of the divine latitude in which, if you are fortunate, you may be able to remain for years.

When the thought flash is the voice of God speaking to an individual, this communication rarely if ever comes in the form of a booming voice, as suggested in melodramatic movie versions of ancient biblical events. Instead, you must be attentive to the "wee small voice" inside your head that is different from ordinary conscious-minded thoughts.

God speaks a universal language in the form of the thought flash so that all human beings of all nations and eras can access this great source of wisdom. All you need in order to receive this guidance is the mindset for receiving it. The mindset is the key. Those who do not understand what a mindset is or how to use it tend to get lost in extraneous, non-productive pursuits. A man with nothing but sex on his mind all day, for example, is not attending to what should be his main business. He should not be surprised, therefore, when others with a higher mindset to succeed leave him behind. The person who is able to control primitive appetites and manage personal priorities is the one who ultimately wins.

Thought flashes can be gathered like wild berries. They can also be cultivated, however, by deliberately establishing an innate connection through a technique I call "courting the silence."

COURTING THE SILENCE

Courting the silence is a type of casual but deliberate meditative state in which you do not actually attempt to connect with the Innate to squeeze out thought flashes. Instead, you simply establish a receptive mindset that allows you to recognize and take advantage of a peaceful, uncluttered state of mind in which it does occur. As you inwardly listen, you will find that every now and then the chatter of thought and ideas stops. When your inner attunement connects, a space of silence occurs. You then meditate carefully to observe and experience the silence.

As you observe your inner mental processes for longer periods of time, you notice that, with attention, the "silent bands" in your mind grow increasingly longer. You experience the gap in the mental chatter and then, as you continue to court this silence, the silence grows stronger. The more you listen to this silence, the more there is to listen to, and the first thing you know, you can go for days, weeks, months and years in the silence. It is then, with the proper mindset, that innate thought flash directional signals can become a habit of everyday life, as you begin doing God's will continuously as never before.

MINDSET

The term "mindset" is crucial to the overall philosophy of Lasting Purpose. It is sometimes used interchangeably with "made-up mind," which is a more colloquial term I have used from time to time since my youth. A mindset indicates an irreversible decision to proceed in a certain direction. If a person has a mindset to be wealthy, for example, he or she persists in that direction, ignoring or overcoming all obstacles until that mindset is accomplished. Whether you are playing sports, selling goods and services or pursuing some other goal, having a mindset for its achievement is essential to success. A focused mindset usually produces its own thought flashes, which are to be believed, courted and acted upon.

PERSISTENCY

A focused mindset encourages persistency. When you are persistent, you keep on going in spite of hardships and discouragements, and this helps you to become even more persistent. If you experience a temporary failure, you get up and try again. Persistency keeps you trying until you finally succeed, especially if you persist just for the sake of persisting. You would do well to practice persistency in all endeavors in order to fully develop this valuable natural resource. When you are "persistent just for the sake of being persistent," this trait becomes a habit which, when coupled with the habits of loving just for the sake of loving and doing just for the sake of doing, insures consistent success. Persistency often enables the less talented person to win against potentially more competitive individuals who, having failed to develop this valuable skill, give up before they reach their goal.

AFFIRMATIONS

"I can, I will, I must!" is a shorthand representation of a great variety of positive affirmations which, when spoken with authority, are used to help increase motivation and generate the belief that the envisioned goal will be achieved.

"I must" usually is drawn upon only in times of desperation, when doubt and misgivings begin to creep into your mind to threaten your belief. To overcome this dangerous hurdle, recognizing and reaffirming willingness to pay the price strengthens belief and leads to victory. Every worthwhile goal has a price; people looking for something for nothing usually get nothing for something. Achievement requires focused and persistent hard work, usually without immediate pay or recognition. My motto, learned first from my mother decades ago and later reinforced by B.J. Palmer, continues to be: "Keep on keeping on!"

SPEAKING WITH AUTHORITY

Speaking with authority is a unique, proprietary strategy that I have developed over the years to generate belief. I discovered that, as you repeat affirmations to yourself with just the right tone, timbre and cadence, the authority of the voice generates firm belief in what is being said. Without the magic ingredient of authority, simple affirmations are of little value, and no belief is generated. Belief is the magic ingredient that activates the spiritual eye—the mind's eye—and allows you to visualize that which you want to do.

ACTING AS IF

Speaking with authority can be made even more effective by acting as if. In addition to saying authoritatively what you want your reality to be, you begin to act as if that reality already is in existence. If you desire to be brave, as you speak with authority, telling yourself that you are brave, you also begin acting as if you have great courage. This total belief package of speaking, acting and visualizing is very effective in generating material resources, as well as in attracting the human resources from others to assure your continued progress toward your goals and objectives.

INNER EYE

Once belief has been accomplished, a vision of an objective being achieved can be seen in your mind's eye—a term used interchangeably with "spiritual eye" and "inner eye." The Bible says, "All things are possible to those who believe." The secret is in learning how to speak with authority to yourself, so that the object of your desire becomes believable in your mind. Then you have the ability to believe and to create visions and ideas, and you can understand the direction you need to go. Even though you may not be able to see into the distant future to know exactly what the turn of events will be, you nevertheless know that you have the ability to achieve and that you will meet each challenge and do whatever is necessary to reach your objective. You are able to see things not as they are, but as they could be and as you would have them be.

LASTING PURPOSE

"Lasting Purpose" is an overall term for a philosophy that advocates the establishment of a mindset for loving, serving and giving out of your own abundance, just for the sake of doing so and with no ulterior motives in mind. This habit produces an atmosphere of support and cooperation among others and thus helps to attract the ideas, people and other resources required for achieving.

A commitment to Lasting Purpose helps to build the human resources of love and persistency. While physical resources are depleted by use, these human resources are increased with use.

A map of a wilderness can give you a general idea of where you should go, but it cannot forewarn you of every storm or every encounter with danger. Neither can it always alert you to the most delicious fruits or the sweetest water along the way. To fully know, you must apply the principles and live the Lasting Purpose life yourself.

About the Author

Sid E. Williams, D.C., is the founder and president of the world's largest chiropractic college, Life College in Marietta, Georgia. He also founded Life Chiropractic College West in San Lorenzo, California, and serves as chancellor of both institutions.

Dr. Williams has long been active in state, national and international affairs dealing with the chiropractic profession. He is a former president of the International Chiropractors Association (ICA), the oldest professional chiropractic association. In 1985, ICA named him the association's "Chiropractor of the Year." A Fellow in the International Chiropractors Association since 1960, he has been elected three times to serve as its chairman of the board. Dr. Williams also sits on the board of the Council on Chiropractic Education, the official agency whose Commission of Accreditation is recognized by the U.S. Department of Education.

Dr. Williams is a prolific writer, addressing health and wellness, professional development, leadership and personal motivation issues. He established the chiropractic profession's leading magazine, *Today's Chiropractic*, which is published by Life College. He is creator of the highly successful Dynamic Essentials seminar program, which instructs professionals and laypersons alike in the principles and practices of chiropractic. A recognized authority in his field, Dr. Williams has promoted his philosophy of health and success for over 30 years.